BLUEPRINT TO MAKE BHARAT VISHWAGURU

VARAD TIKAM

Made with ♥ on the Notion Press Platform
www.notionpress.com

To the Almighty Shakti,
In deep gratitude and reverence, I dedicate this book to You. Your divine
guidance and strength have illuminated my path and enabled me to
envision a greater future for Bharat.

Thank you for blessing me with the clarity and resolve to pursue this
vision of making Bharat a Vishwaguru. This book is a testament to Your
grace and an offering of my dedication to our nation's growth and
potential.

With heartfelt thanks,
Varad Tikam

Contents

Contents

Foreword

As the author of BluePrint to Make Bharat Vishwaguru, I am honored to introduce you to a work that has been a year in the making, shaped by my vision and dedication to our nation's future.

This book is more than just a collection of ideas; it is a blueprint for a brighter, more prosperous Bharat. It reflects my belief that India, with its rich heritage and immense potential, can emerge as a global leader, a Vishwaguru. The ideas presented here are rooted in a deep understanding of our strengths and challenges, and they are intended to offer practical solutions that can drive real change.

Writing this book has been a journey of exploration and transformation. I have poured my heart and soul into every page, driven by a passion to see Bharat thrive and lead with wisdom and innovation. My hope is that the insights and proposals in this book will inspire and empower you, as they have inspired me.

I invite you to join me in this journey of discovery and progress. Together, let us work towards a future where Bharat stands as a beacon of knowledge, leadership, and prosperity.

Thank you for embarking on this journey with me.

Warm regards,

Varad Tikam

Acknowledgements

Writing BluePrint to Make Bharat Vishwaguru has been a profound journey, and I am deeply grateful to all who have supported and guided me along the way.

First and foremost, I extend my heartfelt thanks to the Almighty Shakti, whose divine guidance and strength have illuminated my path and granted me the vision to pursue this ambitious project.

To my family and friends, your unwavering support and encouragement have been a source of inspiration. Your belief in my vision and your patience during the countless hours of writing and revising have been invaluable.

I also wish to acknowledge the wider community of readers, thinkers, and leaders who strive for progress and transformation in Bharat. Your dedication and passion for a better future have been a constant motivation for me.

Warmest regards,
Varad Tikam

Invocation Of The Almigthy

Before we embark on this journey to envision and realize Bharat as a Vishvaguru, let us first invoke the blessings of the Almighty. In this pursuit of wisdom, strength, and unity, it is only fitting that we begin by seeking divine guidance.

"ॐ एकदन्ताय विद्महे वक्रतुंडाय धीमहि तन्नो बुद्धि प्रचोदयात ।
"

"कृष्णाय वासुदेवाय हरये परमात्मने । प्रणतः क्लेशनाशाय गोविदाय नमो नमः
।
"

"ॐ त्र्यम्बकं यजामहे सुगन्धिं पुष्टिवर्धनम् । उर्वारुकमिव बन्धनान्
मृत्योर्मुक्षीय मामृतात् ॥
काल हर ॥ कष्ट हर ॥ दुख हर ॥ दारिद्द हर ॥ सर्व पाप हर ॥ नमः
पार्वती पतये हर हर महादेव ॥"

CHAPTER ONE

KNOW THE AUTHOR BEFORE THE BOOK

"कृष्णाय वासुदेवाय हरये परमात्मने । प्रणतः क्लेशनाशाय गोवदिाय नमो नमः ।"

Dear Reader,

Before we dive into the depths of this book, I'd like to take a moment to introduce myself and share a bit about who I am. My name is Varad Tikam, and the journey that has led me to write "BluePrint to Make Bharat Vishwaguru" is one of deep reflection, dedication, and passion for our nation.

At the time of writing this book, I am a young author with big dreams for my country. As one of the youngest authors in India, I've poured my heart and soul into this work, driven by a vision of growth and progress for both myself and Bharat. My professional path has been diverse, encompassing various roles and experiences that have shaped my understanding of India's potential and challenges. From running a drop servicing agency named Zepious to engaging deeply with critical issues in my writing, each experience has been a stepping stone towards this endeavor.

I have always believed that Bharat (India) holds immense potential to be a global leader, a Vishwaguru, guiding the world with its rich heritage and innovative spirit. This belief has motivated me to explore various facets of our nation's strengths and weaknesses and to develop a comprehensive plan that addresses these areas. Through this book, I aim to offer a blueprint that not only highlights the path to becoming a Vishwaguru but also provides actionable solutions to the challenges we face.

In my professional journey, I've had the privilege of engaging with various aspects of India's socio-economic and political landscape. This book is not just a compilation of ideas but a culmination of extensive research, analysis, and a sincere desire to see Bharat reach its full potential. It reflects my conviction that India can lead with wisdom and strength, provided we have a clear vision and actionable strategies.

As you read through the chapters, you will see that this book is more than just theoretical concepts; it's a practical guide with a focus on implementing ideas that can drive real change. I must also mention that, as a young author, I have taken precautions to avoid any legal complications. To this end, I have beeped out the names of individuals, firms, political parties, and other entities. This is not to shy away from the truth but to protect my work and focus on the bigger picture.

I invite you to join me on this journey of exploration and transformation, and I hope that the insights shared in these pages will inspire and empower us all to work towards making Bharat Vishwaguru.

Thank you for embarking on this journey with me.

Warm regards,

Varad Tikam

THE 1% TAX SYSTEM

Introduction

India stands on the cusp of a new era, where the choices we make today will define our nation's future. As our country grows and evolves, so does the need for a tax system that not only supports this growth but also ensures that every citizen is part of the journey. The current tax regime, with its heavy reliance on a small segment of the population, is both unsustainable and inequitable. The burden on the middle class has reached a point where it is no longer just a financial strain but a source of widespread frustration and discontent. To address this, we must rethink our approach to taxation, creating a system that is fair, inclusive, and capable of generating the necessary funds for our most critical needs, particularly in research and development (R&D). This is where the concept of a 1% tax comes into play—a simple yet powerful idea that can transform India's economic landscape by ensuring that every citizen contributes to the nation's progress, no matter how small the amount.

Understanding the 1% Tax

The 1% tax system is based on a simple yet powerful premise: every individual who earns income will contribute a small, fixed percentage—1%—of their earnings to the government as tax. For instance, if a person earns ₹1000, they will pay ₹10 as tax. While this may seem like a nominal amount, when multiplied across India's population of over 1.4 billion people, the potential for revenue generation is immense. This tax model is designed to be universally applicable, ensuring that every citizen, regardless of their income level, contributes to the nation's financial pool.

The simplicity of this system is one of its greatest strengths. By setting the tax rate at a mere 1%, the financial burden on individuals is minimized, making it a feasible and painless contribution for the majority of the population. This approach also eliminates the complexities often associated with progressive tax systems, where higher earners are taxed at disproportionately higher rates. Instead, the 1% tax creates a flat, uniform rate that is easy to understand and administer, reducing the scope for tax evasion and increasing compliance.

The Mechanics of the 1% Tax System

The implementation of the 1% tax would require minimal changes to the existing tax infrastructure, making it a practical and cost-effective reform. The tax would be deducted at the source for salaried individuals, similar to the current Tax Deducted at Source (TDS) system. For self-employed individuals and businesses, the tax would be calculated and paid as part of their regular income tax filing. The key difference lies in the uniformity and scale of the tax, which, when applied across the entire population, would generate a significant and steady stream of revenue.

In conjunction with the 1% tax, the existing tax system would be retained but with restructured tax slabs to ensure a more equitable distribution of the tax burden. The restructuring would aim to prevent the middle class from being disproportionately affected, while ensuring that higher income groups also contribute their fair share. This approach not only lightens the load on the middle class but also promotes fairness by requiring the wealthy to participate more equitably in supporting national development.

One of the most important aspects of the 1% tax system is its potential to broaden the tax base. Currently, a relatively small percentage of India's population pays income tax, leading to an over-reliance on this group for revenue. This creates a disproportionate burden on the middle class, who often feel they are shouldering the weight of the nation's financial needs without receiving equivalent benefits. The popular saying, *"The poor get something, the rich get many things, but the middle class gets the middle finger"* aptly captures this sentiment of frustration. The 1% tax system seeks to address this imbalance by ensuring that everyone contributes, thereby lightening the load on any single group and fostering a sense of shared responsibility.

The funds collected through this system would be earmarked specifically for sectors that are crucial to India's long-term growth, with a particular emphasis on R&D. R&D is the backbone of innovation, driving advancements in technology, healthcare, agriculture, and other critical areas. By investing in R&D, India can develop homegrown solutions to its unique challenges, reduce its dependence on foreign technology, and position itself as a leader in the global knowledge economy. The 1% tax would provide a reliable source of funding for R&D initiatives, enabling sustained investment in projects that have the potential to transform the country's economic landscape.

The Need for the 1% Tax

The rationale behind the 1% tax system is rooted in the urgent need to reform India's tax structure to better align with the country's economic goals. India's current tax system is not equipped to meet the demands of a rapidly growing economy. With a relatively low tax-to-GDP ratio compared to other emerging economies, India struggles to generate sufficient revenue to fund its development needs. This shortfall is particularly evident in the area of R&D, where investment is critical to fostering innovation and driving long-term economic growth.

In the global context, countries that have successfully transitioned to high-income status have done so by investing heavily in R&D. For India to follow a similar path, it must prioritize R&D funding, and the 1% tax offers a sustainable way to achieve this. By broadening the tax base and ensuring that every citizen contributes, the government can generate the necessary funds to support cutting-edge research and development projects. These projects will not only enhance India's technological capabilities but also create new industries, generate employment, and improve the overall quality of life for its citizens.

Moreover, the 1% tax addresses the issue of economic inequality by redistributing the tax burden more equitably. In the current system, the middle class often bears a disproportionate share of the tax load, while the wealthy have access to various means of tax avoidance. By implementing a flat 1% tax, the system becomes more transparent and fair, ensuring that everyone pays their fair share. This approach also has the potential to reduce social tensions and promote a sense of unity, as all citizens participate in the nation's development.

The restructuring of the existing tax slabs alongside the introduction of the 1% tax would further ensure that the middle class is no longer the only group bearing the brunt of taxation. This dual approach creates a balanced system where every income group contributes according to their capacity, thus alleviating the disproportionate burden that has historically fallen on the middle class.

The Broader Impact on India's Economy

The introduction of the 1% tax system would have far-reaching implications for India's economy. Firstly, it would significantly increase the government's revenue, providing much-needed funds for public infrastructure, social welfare programs, and other critical areas. This would enable the government to make strategic investments in sectors that are essential for sustainable growth, such as education, healthcare, and renewable energy. These investments, in turn, would stimulate economic activity, create jobs, and improve living standards across the country.

Secondly, the 1% tax would enhance India's fiscal stability by creating a more predictable and reliable revenue stream. This stability is crucial for long-term planning and investment, as it allows the government to allocate resources more effectively and respond to economic challenges with greater flexibility. By reducing the reliance on a narrow tax base, the 1% tax also mitigates the risks associated with economic downturns, as the broader base ensures that revenue generation remains stable even during periods of economic uncertainty.

Thirdly, the focus on R&D funding would have a transformative impact on India's industrial landscape. By nurturing innovation and supporting the development of new technologies, the 1% tax would help India move up the value chain in global markets. This would not only boost the country's export potential but also attract foreign investment, as companies seek to capitalize on India's growing technological prowess. The resulting economic growth would create a virtuous cycle, where increased revenue from the 1% tax further fuels investment in R&D, driving continuous innovation and development.

Conclusion

As I reflect on the 1% tax system, I am struck by the profound responsibility we have as a nation to create a fair and sustainable future. This chapter is not just an exploration of a new tax system; it's a call to action for every Indian to recognize their role in the country's progress. The 1% tax is more than a policy proposal—it's a vision for a united India where every citizen, regardless of their financial standing, contributes to the nation's growth. This plan is personal to me because it embodies the belief that we can achieve greatness when we all share the burden and benefits of our development.

The middle class, which has often felt neglected and overburdened, deserves a system that respects their contributions and offers them a fair share in the nation's prosperity. By implementing this 1% tax and restructuring the existing tax slabs, we can alleviate the pressures on this vital segment of our society and ensure that everyone, from the poorest to the wealthiest, is invested in India's future. This system is not just about revenue; it's about building a nation where progress is a collective effort, and everyone has a stake in the outcome.

As the author of this vision, I am driven by the belief that India's best days are ahead of us, but only if we are bold enough to rethink our approach to taxation and development. This 1% tax system is a step towards realizing that future—a future where innovation, equity, and shared responsibility are the cornerstones of our national identity. The road ahead is challenging, but with this plan, I am confident that we can create a more prosperous and just India for generations to come.

CHAPTER THREE

Sexual Violence A Big Problem of India

Introduction

Rape is a deeply traumatic and pervasive crime that affects individuals and communities worldwide. Rape is a profound violation of human dignity and a serious crime that transcends cultural, social, and geographical boundaries. It inflicts severe physical, psychological, and emotional trauma on its victims, leaving lasting scars that can impact every aspect of their lives. Despite the progress made in various aspects of human rights and gender equality, rape remains a pervasive and distressingly common occurrence across the globe. The purpose of this chapter is to delve into the multifaceted nature of rape, exploring its underlying causes, the circumstances in which it most frequently occurs, and the urgent need for effective measures to prevent it.

Rape is a grave violation of human rights that demands urgent and sustained action. By understanding the root causes and the contexts in which rape occurs, we can begin to address the underlying issues that perpetuate this crime. Through robust legal frameworks, supportive services for survivors, and a societal shift in attitudes, it is possible to create a world where rape is not tolerated, and survivors are empowered to seek justice and healing. This chapter aims to shed light on the complexities of rape and highlight the critical steps needed to prevent it, ensuring a safer and more equitable world for all.

Misconception

A prevalent and damaging misconception about rape is that it exclusively affects women and girls, while in reality, men and boys are also victims of this heinous crime. This myth perpetuates a culture of silence and stigma, discouraging male survivors from coming forward and seeking justice. Societal notions of masculinity often suggest that men should be impervious to such violations, further compounding their sense of shame and isolation. Unfortunately, this issue is compounded by legal frameworks that fail to address the full spectrum of rape victims. For instance, in India, Section 375 of the Indian Penal Code defines rape narrowly as "sexual intercourse with a woman against her will, without her consent, by coercion, misrepresentation or fraud or at a time when she has been intoxicated or duped or is of unsound mental health and in any case if she is under 18 years of age." This definition excludes men from being recognized as rape victims and offers no legal protection or recourse for male survivors. This gap in the law highlights a critical need for reform, underscoring that rape is a grave violation of human rights regardless of the victim's gender. Ensuring that the legal system acknowledges and addresses the experiences of all survivors is essential for delivering justice and support to everyone affected by sexual violence.

In a disturbing case from Uttar Pradesh, a 37-year-old shopkeeper was arrested for allegedly drugging and sexually assaulting six young males over seven months. The victims, aged between 10 and 23, were reportedly lured to the perpetrator's home, given sedative-laced drinks, and then assaulted. The crime was exposed only after one of the survivors leaked videos of the assaults to the media.

The shopkeeper had installed CCTV cameras in a room of his house to record the assaults, using the footage to blackmail the victims into silence. Following several police raids, he was caught, and a formal complaint was lodged by the mother of one of the survivors.

An FIR was registered under various sections of the Indian Penal Code (IPC) and the Protection of Children from Sexual Offences (POSCO) Act. However, the legal framework in India, particularly under the new Bharatiya Nyaya Sanhita (BNS) law, does not adequately address sexual violence against men and transgender individuals. The introduction of the

BNS in 2024 omitted crucial protections for these victims. While it focuses on offences against women and children, it lacks specific legal provisions to safeguard men and transgender individuals from rape and sexual violence. The removal of Section 377 of the IPC, which previously addressed non-consensual penile penetrative sex, has created a legal void, leaving male and transgender victims without clear protection.

What causes rapes?

One approach to acquire an answer is to ask a rapist directly. This is what Madhumita Pandey did. Madhumita discovered that many rapists believe this. "I am not a rapist." "Yes, I had sex, I did not take consent for it." Or, "'what is consent? '" "Or "No, I was not sure that she was saying no. '" She questioned a 49-year-old rapist who had raped a 5-year-old child and asked him why. Madhumita was stunned by his response. The rapist said that the child's 'character' was awful, and hence she ought to be punished. Madhumita inquired as to if he felt terrible. The rapist said that he felt awful. Because he destroyed her life. She is no longer a virgin, thus no one no one will marry her. But he is willing to marry her after serving his sentence. This is a very a disturbing statement. This offered us insight into the mindset of a rapist. That the rapist felt awful, not because he raped the child, but because the girl may not be able to marry as a result of this. This demonstrates the perspective through which rapists view society. Many people questioned numerous rapists if they had forced themselves on their victims, and all of them responded yes. They inquired if they had raped the victims, and they denied it. According to my findings, rapists feel no regret. Rather, they blame the victims.

This is referred to as cognitive distortion. Jaydip Sarkar conducted a mental health analysis of several rapists. Many rapists felt that when a man's sexual desire reaches a hazardous level, it is important to fulfill it. Some rapists said that if their sperm goes to waste, they will grow feeble. And, to avoid this vulnerability, a female should give herself. You must have been stunned to hear these things. According to researchers, this tendency can be explained by two possibilities. Evolutionary theory and societal theory. In 1968, psychiatrist James A. Brussel remarked that "Nobody is born to commit rape, however, the potential for Rape is in every person." Why is he saying this? Because many psychologists think that a person reproduces for evolutionary reasons.

Charles Darwin proposed the Theory of Evolution many years ago.He believed that all organisms choose their mate based on many specific physical traits. That's why many animals fight each other before mating with a female. So that the female is convinced that the male organism she chooses is strong. Charles Darwin says that humans do this too. A woman chooses a man with a strong build so that he can protect her and her children Men like women with bigger hips and breasts, which are signs of fertility. According to evolutionary theory, every organism's objective is to spread its gene, which may include dangerous behaviour. People who use evolutionary theory to describe the psychology of rapists argue that they are all motivated by the same objective. The majority of Rapevictims are between the ages of 18-30.

According to data from 2022, this age group accounted for 66% of all casualties in India. However, this evolutionary hypothesis fails in numerous circumstances. For example, in 2022, 112 females under the age of 12 were raped. Over a thousand ladies over the age of 45 were also raped. These ladies were not at their most fertile. That is why many scholars suggest that depending on evolutionary theory is a societal justification for claiming that the civilization isn't defective, but rather human people as a whole are. In contrast, the Socio-Cultural theory suggests that a man is driven to be a rapist because of his society.

Mukesh Singh was a convicted rapist in the Nirbhaya case. In 2012, on a December night, on a moving bus, a girl named Nirbhaya was raped. "It takes two hands to clap. You can't refute that. A 'proper' girl wouldn't be out at 9 PM." Had such views but where as Our society also holds similar views. "You can't clap with one hand. The boy and the girl know each other, they have an understanding, Otherwise, such things don't happen. " That's why many people blame the society. Many individuals believe that rapes occur because males in our culture are sexually deprived. They have unsatisfied sexual cravings. But Madhumita and other academics have demonstrated that this is wrong. Rapeisn't about sex. Rapeis about power and dominance. Rapeis a tactic that boys use to manipulate girls.

Many political leaders have similar traditional beliefs. "They're boys, boys make mistakes." "Why should they be hanged?" M.S Ya**v (Indian politician) stated that "boys make errors." They should not be hanged for it. In 2012, M. Bhagw**t Chief of a 'Hindu discipline organisation' stated that "rapes occur in India, not Bharat". According to M Bhag**t, such crimes are rare in Bharat but common in India.

It may be translated as "If girls do traditional things, they will be safe." However, when they want to be modern, wear revealing clothes, start earning money, and enter society, the troubles begin. When girls did not wear such clothing, there were no rape incidents.

One of the most common lines you must have heard is "If a girl wears such clothes, of course, she'll be raped. " or "If they wear revealing clothes, anyone would be tempted."
However, the primary cause for all of this is how society perceives girls. In any patriarchal culture, boys and girls have different privileges. In any patriarchal society, girls are considered weaker. They are unable to think freely. And that is why they must be managed. Let me repeat: these civilizations feel that girls are weak. They are unable to think freely. Thus, they must be regulated. If they are not supervised, they will make mistakes.

When the desire to dominate females gets too strong, it leads to sexual assault. There are several examples of this control in our society. For example, even today, 80% of women must obtain permission before attending a health facility. Almost half of the ladies do not leave their houses even once each day. One unique aspect of patriarchy is that many women accept these beliefs as well. This is why 29% of Indian women feel that a husband may beat his wife if she leaves the house without his permission. 14% of women believe a husband may slap his wife if she refuses to have sex.

Sexual violence is more than simply overpowering girls; it also conveys a message to others. For example, following the split, sexual violence was utilised to denigrate the other group. We witnessed this in Manipur, as well as in Myanmar's Rohingya atrocities. Girls and women are suffering.

Many males believe that if ladies are weak, they can overcome it through exposure treatment. That is, if they speak with girls. But this does not happen in our culture, either in schools or at home. Forget about looking at girls. If they are not allowed to talk to the girls in their school, how will the misconceptions in their minds go away? We can see the same thing in schools, Recently (at the time of writing) news went viral that stated CCTV cameras were mounted in the halls of Kendriya Vidhyalay in Bengaluru to monitor if boys and girls were chatting to one other. 95% of Indian schools are coeducational. However, guys and girls are not permitted to sit together. Because there is a significant difference between boys and girls throughout childhood, it is simple for misunderstandings to get normalized in their thoughts. This is why many males believe that when a girl smiles, she is attracting their attention.

Solutions according to Varad Tikam

In the quest for justice and the reduction of crime, the debate over the effectiveness of punitive measures is both complex and contentious. One of the most heated discussions revolves around the severity of punishment for heinous crimes, particularly rape. While many advocate for stricter penalties, including capital punishment, evidence and expert opinions suggest that this approach may not be as effective as intended. This chapter explores the multifaceted nature of criminal justice, focusing on the impact of stringent penalties on victims and offenders, and presents an argument for a more nuanced approach to crime deterrence.

1. The Impact of Stricter Penalties on Victims

The notion of implementing stricter punishments, such as the death penalty for rapists, is often driven by the desire to create a strong deterrent against such crimes. However, this approach may inadvertently have detrimental effects on the victims themselves. According to statistics, in approximately 97% of rape cases, the perpetrator is someone known to the victim. This close relationship introduces a significant layer of psychological and social pressure when deciding whether to file a complaint.

Advocate Vrinda Grover has highlighted a critical issue: victims are frequently subjected to immense pressure and stigma, including the fear of ruining their own lives by pursuing legal action. The prospect of severe punishment, such as capital punishment, may exacerbate these fears, leading victims to reconsider reporting the crime. The punitive measure intended to serve justice can thus transform into a burden that discourages victims from seeking redress.

Furthermore, the social repercussions of reporting rape, including societal judgment and personal trauma, can be intensified by the knowledge that the perpetrator faces severe punishment. As a result, stricter penalties might lead to underreporting and a subsequent failure to bring perpetrators to justice.

2. The Risk of Increased Violence

Another critical consideration is the potential unintended consequence of harsher punishments: the increased risk of violence against victims. Activists and experts argue that if the punishment for rape is severe, perpetrators might resort to killing their victims to eliminate witnesses and avoid the severe penalty. The fear of facing a death sentence if caught could lead offenders to commit additional crimes, including murder, to prevent their exposure.

Evidence from various countries supports this concern. Research from 141 nations indicates that the abolition of capital punishment is associated with a decrease in rape cases. This counterintuitive outcome highlights that the fear of severe punishment does not always deter crime. Instead, the likelihood of being caught plays a more significant role in influencing criminal behavior.

3. The Equation of Crime Deterrence

The deterrent effect of punishment is often oversimplified. Criminologist Daniel Nagin argues that increasing the probability of apprehension, rather than the severity of punishment, is more effective in reducing crime. The underlying equation is straightforward: a criminal evaluates both the severity of potential punishment and the likelihood of being caught. While severe penalties might appear to be a strong deterrent, the probability of being caught plays a more critical role in a criminal's decision-making process.

This perspective emphasizes that focusing solely on the severity of punishment without improving the efficiency of law enforcement and judicial processes may be ineffective. Effective crime deterrence requires a balanced approach that addresses both the likelihood of apprehension and the severity of the consequences.

Fake Rape Cases Problems

False rape accusations pose a serious issue in India, undermining the credibility of the legal system and harming innocent individuals. These cases not only erode public trust but also complicate the pursuit of justice for genuine victims of sexual violence. With a significant number of reported cases turning out to be false or misused for personal gain, the problem of fake rape cases diverts attention and resources away from real instances of abuse, making it harder for true victims to be believed and supported. Addressing this issue requires a multifaceted approach, including better legal procedures, educational initiatives, and increased public awareness.

Vishnu Tiwari from Uttar Pradesh faced a major problem. In September 2000, at the age of 23, he was wrongly convicted of rape. Twenty years later, the Allahabad High Court found there wasn't enough evidence for his conviction. Vishnu claimed that the case was actually about a land dispute and that he had never even met the woman who accused him. He believes they just wanted money from him. Sadly, Vishnu's case is not unique.

The issue of false rape accusations is significant. In 2022, there were 45,000 reported rape cases in India, but only 27.5% of these cases ended in a conviction. This means that more than 75% of the cases did not lead to a conviction. One reason could be that victims are pressured to change their statements. Another reason might be that some rape cases are completely false. In a study by data journalist Rukmini Srinivasan in 2013, she found that in 25% of the cases she looked at, parents filed rape charges when their daughters ran away with a boy. Additionally, data from Jaipur showed that 43% of 330 reported rape cases there were false.

Retired Supreme Court Justice B. N. Shrikrishna has pointed out that rape laws are sometimes misused, which undermines trust in the legal system. Because of this misuse, real victims can face skepticism when they try to report rape.

Despite these problems, efforts are being made to address sexual violence in India.

CHAPTER FOUR

REDEFINING THE SANATAN DHRAM

As we envision a Bharat that once again leads the world as a Vishwaguru, it is crucial to re-examine our land's spiritual and philosophical foundations. Hindu, Jain, and Buddhist traditions have coexisted for millennia, often seen as distinct religions. However, these traditions are all expressions of Sanatan Dharm—the eternal way of living. Understanding them as part of one unified tradition will not only strengthen our spiritual identity but also revive the values that once made India the heart of global wisdom.

In this chapter, I will delve deep into the historical, cultural, and philosophical connections that bind these traditions together under the broad umbrella of Sanatan Dharm. By the end of this exploration, it will become clear that these ancient teachings form the core of one cohesive spiritual philosophy. If India is to reclaim its role as a global spiritual leader, this unity must be recognized and promoted for the benefit of future generations.

The Historical Background

Sanatan Dharm, or "the eternal law," has been the spiritual bedrock of Indian civilization for over 5,000 years. It is not a religion in the Western sense, but a way of life grounded in the principles of dhram (righteousness), karam (action), and moksh (liberation). The teachings of Sanatan Dharm are deeply rooted in the Veds, the oldest spiritual texts known to humanity, composed around 1500 BCE. These texts, especially the Rig Ved, contain hymns that reveal the core concepts of an interconnected world, the divine, and human duty.

The concept of Sanatan Dharm was further developed in the Upanishads (circa 800–400 BCE), which introduced the profound philosophies of Atman (self) and Brahman (the ultimate reality). The Upanishads provide a blueprint for spiritual evolution that resonates through Hindu, Jain, and Buddhist teachings. These texts emphasize the realization of one's true self and the pursuit of higher knowledge to achieve liberation (moksh).

To fully understand how Jain and Buddh traditions are part of Sanatan Dharm, it is essential to delve into the schools of thought that have shaped Indian philosophy. These schools, or Darshan, offer a structured understanding of the universe, the self, and the path to liberation. Historically, Indian philosophy has been classified into Astika (orthodox) and Nastika (heterodox) schools. Both Jain and Buddh traditions fall under the Nastika category, but this classification has often been misunderstood. When examined closely, the core principles of these traditions align with the broader framework of Sanatan Dharm, emphasizing dhram, karam, and moksh.

Astik Schools of Thought (Orthodox)

The Astika schools accept the authority of the Veds and form the foundation of what is commonly referred to as Hindu philosophy. They are six in number, and together they reflect different facets of Sanatan Dharm.

Nyay: Founded by Gautama, Nyaya emphasizes logic and epistemology. It is the school of logic that establishes the path to moksh through reasoning and understanding the nature of reality. Jain and Buddh philosophies also utilize extensive logic, particularly in the examination of cause and effect, similar to Nyaya's analysis.

Vaisheshik: Developed by Kanada, Vaisheshika is a naturalist school that focuses on atomism—the idea that everything is made up of atoms and follows the laws of nature. Vaisheshika, much like Jain philosophy, attempts to explain the material world while also addressing metaphysical questions about the soul and liberation.

Samkhy: Attributed to Kapila, Samkhya is a dualistic philosophy that distinguishes between Purusha (consciousness) and Prakriti (matter). Though it does not promote theism, it provides a framework for understanding the mind-body relationship and the importance of transcending worldly attachments. In Jainism, similar distinctions are made between the Jiva (soul) and the Ajiva (non-soul), and the path to liberation also involves detachment from material bonds.

Yog: Patanjali's Yoga is closely aligned with Samkhya, but it emphasizes practical methods for achieving spiritual liberation through physical and mental discipline. The eightfold path of Yoga—known as Ashtanga Yoga—aligns with the spiritual disciplines found in both Jain and Buddh traditions, particularly in their emphasis on self-control, meditation, and the pursuit of inner purity.

Purva Mimams: Founded by Jaimini, Purva Mimamsa emphasizes the performance of Vedic rituals as a means to uphold dhram. While Jain and Buddh schools reject ritualism, they maintain a strong ethical framework, rooted in dhram, which emphasizes right conduct, much like Mimamsa's emphasis on moral duty.

Vedant Badarayana's Vedanta, which interprets the teachings of the Upanishads, is centered on the concept of the ultimate reality, Brahman, and the liberation of the self from the cycle of birth and death. Vedanta's emphasis on non-duality, especially as taught by Adi Shankaracharya's Advaita Vedanta, parallels the non-attachment principles in Jainism and Buddhism, where the ultimate goal is the dissolution of the individual ego and union with a higher reality (moksh).

Nastika Schools of Thought (Heterodox)

The Nastika schools are classified as those that do not accept the authority of the Veds. However, they do not reject the core Sanatan Dharm principles of dhram, karam, and moksh. Jainism and Buddhism fall under this category, along with Charvaka.

Jain Philosophy

Jainism, while categorized as a Nastika school, shares many philosophical principles with the broader framework of Sanatan Dharm. The Jain school was formalized around the teachings of Mahavir, the 24th Tirthankar, but it traces its origins back to earlier Tirthankars like Rishabhnath, who is also mentioned in Hindu scriptures. The primary contributions of Jainism to Indian philosophy include:

Ahimsa (Non-violence): Jainism takes the concept of non-violence to its extreme, advocating not just for physical non-harm but also non-violence in thought and speech. This aligns with the Sanatan concept of dhram, where righteousness and compassion are key.

Anekantavada (Multiplicity of Perspectives): This is the Jain theory that reality can be viewed from multiple perspectives, reflecting the complexity of existence. Anekantavada resonates with the pluralistic approach of Sanatan Dharm, which accommodates various paths to spiritual realization.

Karma and Moksh: Jainism's view of karam and moksh is highly structured. The soul (jiva) accumulates karmic particles through action, and liberation (moksh) is attained through purification and the cessation of karmic bondage. While Jainism rejects the Veds and ritualism, its focus on self-realization and ethical conduct mirrors the goals of Sanatan Dharm.

Buddh Philosophy

Buddh Dharm, founded by Siddhartha Gautama (the Buddha), is another Nastika tradition, yet it is deeply rooted in the same spiritual soil as Sanatan Dharm. Though Buddhists reject the authority of the Veds, the Buddha himself was born into a Kshatriya family practicing Vedic rituals, and many of his teachings align with core Sanatan principles.

The Four Noble Truths and the Eightfold Path: The Four Noble Truths acknowledge the existence of suffering (dukkha), its cause, its cessation, and the path to its cessation. The Eightfold Path provides a practical guide to ethical and mental discipline, similar to the moral imperatives found in Sanatan Dharm. Concepts such as right action, right speech, and right livelihood closely parallel the dhram laid out in the Veds.

Karma and Rebirth: Like Hinduism and Jainism, Buddh Dharm teaches the law of karam and the cycle of rebirth (samsara). The ultimate goal is Nirvana, a state of liberation from the cycle of birth and death. While Buddhism emphasizes the doctrine of Anatman (no-self), it still upholds the Sanatan concept of breaking free from karmic bonds to attain liberation.

Meditation and Detachment: Buddh Dharm places a strong emphasis on meditation and mindfulness, akin to the practices outlined in Yoga. The detachment from desires and the renunciation of ego-driven actions are themes that resonate with the teachings of the Bhagavad Gita and the broader Sanatan tradition.

Charvak

The Charvak school represents the materialist viewpoint and outright rejects concepts such as karma, rebirth, and moksh. Charvaka believed only in direct sensory experience and rejected the existence of an afterlife or spiritual principles. While this school diverges sharply from Sanatan Dharm, its presence in Indian philosophy highlights the broad spectrum of thought that Sanatan Dharm has traditionally accommodated, including dissenting views.

Jain and Buddh Traditions as Branches of Sanatan Dharm

Despite being categorized as Nastika schools, both Jainism and Buddhism share philosophical and ethical principles with the Astika schools of Sanatan Dharm. Their divergence lies primarily in the rejection of Vedic authority and ritualistic practices, yet their ultimate goals—moksh, the cessation of suffering, and the pursuit of dhram—are in harmony with the teachings of Sanatan Dharm.

In redefining Jainism and Buddhism as branches of Sanatan Dharm, it becomes clear that these traditions are not separate religions but reformist movements within the same spiritual ecosystem. They offer complementary perspectives on the nature of existence, ethical conduct, and the path to liberation, enriching the Sanatan tradition with their unique contributions.

Evidence of Shared Roots

There is overwhelming evidence, both historical and archaeological, that demonstrates the shared roots of Hindu, Jain, and Buddh traditions.

The Indus Valley Civilization (circa 2500–1500 BCE), one of the world's earliest urban cultures, has yielded artifacts that suggest common spiritual practices. Seals depicting meditative postures, sacred symbols like the swastika, and yogic postures indicate that early spiritual traditions in India were evolving from a shared cultural context.

Texts such as the Bhagavad Gita (circa 2nd century BCE) demonstrate the philosophical unity between these traditions. For instance, Krishna's teachings on detachment from the fruits of action, found in the Gita, are echoed in the Buddha's discourse on avoiding attachment to worldly desires. This interconnectedness points to a common source of spiritual wisdom.

The early spread of **Buddh Dharm** across India and beyond was often supported by rulers and teachers who also upheld Hindu traditions. The famous Indian emperor Ashoka, who converted to Buddhism in the 3rd century BCE, still adhered to core Sanatan values, promoting dhram, non-violence, and tolerance across his empire.

Problem 1: Fragmentation of Dharma

In modern-day India, a significant issue is the perception of fragmentation within the larger framework of Sanatan Dharm. Jainism, Buddhism, and Hinduism, though sharing deep philosophical roots, are often seen as separate religions. This division creates unnecessary religious, social, and political conflicts. Historically, these traditions emerged from the same cultural and spiritual ethos, but over time, external influences and internal schisms led to their division. The lack of understanding regarding their shared heritage has caused tension and weakened the spiritual unity of Bharat.

In the past, Emperor Ashoka embraced Buddhism after the Kalinga War, leading to the promotion of Buddh Dharm across India and beyond. However, despite Ashoka's efforts to propagate non-violence and compassion, the separation between Buddhists and followers of other schools within Sanatan Dharm became more pronounced over time. This division fostered a sense of religious fragmentation, contributing to political and social divides.

Problem 2: Conversion of Dalits and the Caste System

A major problem plaguing Indian society has been the practice of untouchability and the rigid caste system, which is a distortion of the original Varna system. This distortion led to the marginalization of Dalits, who have historically faced severe discrimination. As a response to this injustice, many Dalits, led by Dr. B.R. Ambedkar, converted to Buddh Dharm in 1956 as a form of resistance against the caste-based oppression entrenched in Hindu society. While Ambedkar promoted Buddhism as a way to reject the caste system, the irony is that both Buddh Dharm and the original Dharmic traditions share the same spiritual roots.

However, in modern India, many Dalits, despite converting to Buddh Dharm, are still classified as Hindus in official records and everyday social contexts. This confusion stems from the artificial divisions imposed by the colonial era and modern political manipulation. The redefining of these Dharmic traditions as part of one unified Sanatan Dharm could restore dignity to Dalits, eliminate the caste system, and unite the people of India.

Dr. Ambedkar, who led the mass conversion of Dalits to Buddhism, emphasized that his adoption of Buddhism was not a rejection of the Indian spiritual tradition but rather a rejection of the hierarchical and oppressive caste system. He sought equality, which he believed was rooted in the Dharmic values of compassion and justice. Despite converting, Dalits today remain intertwined with Hindu practices, leading to identity confusion. A redefinition that emphasizes Sanatan Dharm's inclusiveness could bridge this gap.

Problem 3: Political and Social Division Based on Religion

The rigid distinction between religions has also contributed to political divisions. Different religious identities are often used for vote bank politics, creating unnecessary divisions and animosity. This artificial separation weakens India's unity, hindering its progress toward becoming a global leader. By redefining these traditions as part of a unified Dharmic framework, India could eliminate the false boundaries that divide its people and tap into the collective spiritual and cultural strength that all these traditions share.

In modern times, politicians often use religion to divide voters along communal lines, pitting Hindus, Jains, and Buddhists against one another for electoral gains. However, the shared cultural heritage of these communities could be a powerful unifying force if recognized and celebrated. During the time of Emperor Chandragupta Maurya, Jain and Buddh monks worked together in harmony to guide the spiritual and political direction of the kingdom. Such unity can be restored through redefining these traditions under Sanatan Dharm.

Solutions according to Varad Tikam

Redefining Religion under Sanatan Dharm

The solution lies in understanding that Hinduism, Jainism, and Buddhism are not separate entities but branches of the same ancient spiritual tradition—Sanatan Dharm. The artificial divisions that arose over centuries can be healed by redefining these faiths as different paths leading to the same truth. Sanatan Dharm, in its essence, recognizes multiple paths to spiritual liberation, and by integrating the teachings of Jain, Buddh, and Hindu thought, India can once again unify its people under a common cultural and spiritual banner.

Uniting Dalits with Sanatan Dharm

The redefinition of these Dharmic traditions can provide a solution to the caste issue. Dalits, who converted to Buddhism to escape caste-based discrimination, can be re-integrated into Sanatan Dharm by acknowledging that their chosen path (Buddh Dharm) is an essential part of the Dharmic continuum. By eliminating the false divisions of caste through this redefinition, India can erase centuries of injustice and bring about social harmony.

Educational Reform

India's education system must reintroduce the true history of our spiritual traditions, emphasizing the unity between Hindu, Jain, and Buddhist teachings. This can be achieved through updated curricula that highlight their shared roots in Sanatan Dharm.

Cultural Initiatives

National programs that promote interfaith dialogue among Hindu, Jain, and Buddhist communities should be encouraged. Such initiatives would not only foster harmony but also inspire a renewed understanding of our spiritual heritage.

Legal Recognition

The Indian Constitution should acknowledge Sanatan Dharm as the overarching spiritual tradition that unites Hindu, Jain, and Buddh practices. This could be implemented through legislative amendments that recognize the shared principles of dhram, karam, and moksh across these traditions.

Conclusion

As we move forward in our journey to make Bharat a Vishwaguru, it is vital to restore the unity of our spiritual traditions. The division between Hindus, Jains, and Buddhists is a historical misunderstanding, not a reflection of the true essence of these paths. By redefining religion and embracing Sanatan Dharm as the common ground, we can break the chains of caste and religious fragmentation that have long held us back. This unification will not only heal the social fabric of our nation but also propel us toward our destiny as a global spiritual leader. Together, we can transcend the artificial boundaries of caste and religion and rise as one, united under the timeless wisdom of Sanatan Dharm.

"If you dont know were you came from,You wont' know where you are going."

CHAPTER FIVE

CASTE SYSTEM

As I sit down to pen this chapter, I am reminded of the deep-rooted inequalities that still plague our nation. The caste system, once a fluid structure based on the occupation and contribution of individuals, has become rigid and oppressive over the centuries. This outdated system, which was never meant to define us by birth, continues to divide our society, hindering India's potential as a global leader. To fulfill the dream of making Bharat Vishwaguru, we must dismantle this relic of the past and build an India where every individual, regardless of their caste or background, is given equal opportunity to thrive.

Addressing caste-based violence and discrimination is not just a matter of social justice; it is vital for India's progress and unity. The caste system's stranglehold, especially in rural areas, keeps millions from realizing their full potential. We cannot achieve our goal of becoming a global leader while these injustices persist. It is time to replace caste-based reservations and certificates with a system rooted in merit and economic fairness. Only then can we move forward as one united nation.

The Problem

The caste system, as it exists today, is a perversion of the ancient Varna system. Historically, Varna was a system where individuals were assigned roles based on their profession, not their birth. However, centuries of exploitation and social engineering have turned it into a rigid hierarchy, where certain castes are seen as superior, while others, particularly Dalits and marginalized communities, suffer systemic violence and discrimination.

According to the National Crime Records Bureau (NCRB), in 2022 alone, over **50,000 cases of crimes against Dalits** were reported across India. These crimes range from physical assaults to murders, rapes, and cases of untouchability. One particularly heart-wrenching example occurred in Uttar Pradesh, where a young Dalit girl was brutally raped and murdered, sparking nationwide outrage. Her case, however, was only one of many, as Dalit women face significantly higher rates of sexual violence compared to upper-caste women.

This systemic violence is perpetuated by the very existence of caste certificates, which continue to define individuals based on their caste, reinforcing societal hierarchies. While reservations have helped uplift certain communities, they have also perpetuated division by cementing caste identities. The time has come to ask ourselves: Is this how we want to define the future of India?

Solutions according to Varad Tikam

Abolish Caste Certificates and Shift to Merit-Based Systems

To eradicate the caste system, the first step is to abolish caste certificates. These documents, which label individuals by their caste, should be declared obsolete. Instead of perpetuating division, the government should introduce a system where individuals are recognized for their talents, skills, and economic background. A constitutional amendment can declare caste certificates as non-essential, thereby removing their significance in public life.

This shift will create a society where an individual's worth is no longer tied to their caste but to their merit and contributions. The modern caste system has deviated so far from its original intent that it serves no useful purpose. By recognizing this fact and abolishing caste-based identities, we can take a significant step toward creating a more unified India.

Replace Caste-Based Reservations with Economic-Based Support

Currently, reservations in India are based primarily on caste. While this was necessary in the past to uplift marginalized communities, it is time to shift focus. A more equitable system would prioritize those who are economically disadvantaged, regardless of their caste. By introducing **Economic Backward Class (EBC)** reservations, we ensure that opportunities are given to those who need them the most, regardless of their caste or religion.

For example, consider the case of a bright student from an economically poor family in Maharashtra who was denied a college seat despite having high scores, solely because he belonged to an upper caste. Meanwhile, another student from a wealthier family but a reserved caste received a seat due to the reservation system. Such cases highlight the need for reform. By making reservations based on economic status, we address poverty at its root and provide equal opportunities for all.

This transition would not be without challenges. The current caste-based reservation system has its advocates, and resistance is expected. To address this, a phased approach can be taken. First, offer incentives to those who voluntarily give up caste-based reservations. Gradually, as economic reservations take precedence, the country will naturally move away from caste-based divisions.

Educate and Empower Communities to Challenge Caste-Based Violence

A legal framework alone cannot eradicate caste-based violence. Education must play a central role. Schools must integrate lessons on the Varna system, explaining how it was originally based on merit and occupation rather than birth. Furthermore, we must teach young Indians that all individuals, regardless of caste, deserve respect and equality.

In Tamil Nadu, a group of young Dalit activists formed a community organization to educate rural populations about their legal rights and fight against caste-based atrocities. Their work led to a 20% decrease in caste-related violence in the region over five years. Such examples illustrate how empowering local communities can create lasting change.

The government must invest in programs that promote social harmony, support victims of caste-based violence, and encourage reporting of such crimes. Simultaneously, law enforcement agencies must be trained to handle caste-related cases with sensitivity and ensure that justice is delivered swiftly.

Legislative Draft: Amendment to Abolish Caste Certificates

In the spirit of national unity and progress, I propose a constitutional amendment to formally abolish caste certificates and all forms of legal recognition of caste. The draft of this amendment would read:

"The Republic of India recognizes no caste identity in the issuance of official documents or the provision of public services. All citizens shall be entitled to equal treatment under the law, irrespective of their caste or background. Caste certificates shall no longer be issued or required for access to government services, education, or employment opportunities."

This amendment would be accompanied by a bill to introduce Economic Backward Class (EBC) reservations, ensuring that economic disadvantage is prioritized in the allocation of government resources, education seats, and job opportunities.

Conclusion

The time has come to rid India of the shackles of the caste system. I believe that if we can abolish caste certificates and replace caste-based reservations with economic-based ones, we will create a nation that is truly united, where every individual has an equal opportunity to succeed. We cannot allow the divisions of the past to dictate our future.

As I reflect on the immense potential of this great nation, I am reminded of our responsibility to each other. We must rise above the barriers of caste and embrace the principles of equality, justice, and merit. Only then can Bharat truly become Vishwaguru — a global leader, admired for its social harmony and progress. It is time to take bold steps toward an India where everyone, regardless of their background, has the chance to thrive. Together, we will build a future that is brighter, stronger, and more united than ever before.

"*Together, we will rise above the past and build a future where every Indian thrives on merit, equality, and unity.*"

1975 EMERGENCY [ALMOST DICTATORSHIP]

One of the darkest periods in India's history, the **1975 Emergency**, it became clear to me that the line between democracy and dictatorship can blur frighteningly fast. This chapter, titled *1975 Emergency [Almost Dictatorship]*, is not just a recount of events, but a deep dive into how our nation came perilously close to losing its democratic soul. Why do I call it an "almost dictatorship"? The answer lies in the story I tell here—a narrative that takes you through how Indira Gandhi exploited the system, manipulated the Constitution, and nearly succeeded in turning herself into an all-powerful dictator.

But history is a teacher, and as the saying goes, "**wise men learn from the mistakes of the past.**" This chapter not only tells the story of how the Emergency unfolded but also serves as a reminder of what could have been. More importantly, it offers the **solutions** we need to ensure that such a breach of power never happens again. By understanding how our democracy was put in jeopardy, we can take the necessary steps to safeguard it for future generations.

In the final section of this chapter, I propose legal and constitutional reforms that are essential to prevent another Emergency from ever escalating into dictatorship. These solutions are drawn from the lessons learned during this dangerous period of our history, ensuring that the rights of citizens remain protected and that no leader can ever again amass unchecked power.

This chapter is not just about the past—it is about the future, and how we, as a nation, can prevent history from repeating itself.

The Story of 1975 Emergency: When India Almost Lost Its Freedom

The year was 1975. India was reeling under rising inflation, unemployment, and social unrest. The ruling Congress government, led by Prime Minister Indira Gandhi, faced severe criticism from the opposition, and discontent was spreading across the nation. Among the growing voices of resistance was a socialist leader named Jayaprakash Narayan (JP), who called for a "total revolution" against corruption and injustice. The movement, growing in strength, rattled Indira Gandhi's government.

Indira, who had once been hailed as the Iron Lady for her tough stance on issues like the Bangladesh Liberation War, now found herself in a precarious position. Her political future was hanging by a thread, but it was a judicial ruling that sent her over the edge. In June 1975, the Allahabad High Court declared Indira guilty of corrupt practices in the 1971 elections and disqualified her from holding office for six years. The verdict shook the government to its core.

Faced with the possibility of losing power, Indira Gandhi made a drastic decision. On the night of June 25, 1975, she declared a nationwide Emergency, citing internal disturbances. The announcement was made over All India Radio, and by dawn, India's democracy was no longer recognizable. The Emergency had begun.

A Nation in Chains

With the flick of a pen, Indira Gandhi assumed near-total control over the country. Opposition leaders were arrested overnight; among them were political stalwarts like Morarji Desai, Atal Bihari Vajpayee, and George Fernandes. Those who could not be captured immediately went into hiding, but their families were harassed and intimidated. The nation's jails were soon overflowing with political prisoners—many of whom had never committed any crime other than opposing Indira's rule.

Media censorship was imposed. Newspapers could no longer publish stories critical of the government without approval. The country's press, once free and vibrant, was muzzled under the strict control of Indira's regime. To distract the public from the horrors unfolding, the government used state media to broadcast entertainment, including the popular movie *Bobby*, to keep the masses pacified. The real stories—of torture, mass arrests, and repression—were hidden from view.

The Emergency wasn't just about suppressing political opposition. Indira's son, Sanjay Gandhi, who had no official position but wielded enormous power, took charge of the government's notorious sterilization campaign. Under this program, millions of men were forcibly sterilized to control population growth, a plan that quickly turned into a grotesque human rights violation. Ordinary citizens—regardless of whether they were married or single—were rounded up from the streets and sterilized in unhygienic conditions, leading to infections, and in some cases, death. The brutality of this campaign shook the nation.

The Distortion of Democracy

One of the most disturbing aspects of Indira Gandhi's Emergency was how she manipulated the very foundation of India's democracy—the Constitution—to serve her own interests. By altering key constitutional provisions, she systematically dismantled the checks and balances that protected the nation from authoritarian rule. Through a series of amendments, Indira Gandhi ensured that the powers of the Prime Minister and the central government were vastly expanded, effectively rendering India's judiciary and legislative bodies powerless.

The **39th Constitutional Amendment** passed in 1975, was the first significant move in this direction. This amendment was specifically designed to protect Indira Gandhi herself. The Allahabad High Court had found her guilty of electoral malpractices and disqualified her from holding office, but instead of stepping down, she amended the Constitution to prevent the judiciary from having any jurisdiction over the election disputes involving the Prime Minister. It was a blatant power grab, executed with the sole purpose of securing her position.

This was followed by the **42nd Constitutional Amendment** in 1976, which is often called the "Mini-Constitution" because of its sweeping changes. Through this amendment, Indira Gandhi cemented her grip on the country by drastically altering the power structure. The amendment gave the central government unprecedented control over the states, allowing them to override state laws and deploy central forces at will. The

Parliament's and state assemblies' terms were extended from 5 to 6 years, delaying elections and giving her government a longer, unchecked rule.

Perhaps the most shocking change was the suspension of fundamental rights. Under the guise of maintaining order during the Emergency, the amendment allowed the government to suspend the rights of citizens, including the right to life and personal liberty. People could be detained without trial, and there was no recourse to the courts. Judicial review, one of the cornerstones of Indian democracy, was effectively neutralized. The government's actions could no longer be challenged, as laws placed under the Ninth Schedule were immune from judicial scrutiny.

Indira Gandhi's manipulation didn't stop at consolidating power—she also sought to change the very ideology of the nation. By adding the words **"socialist"** and **"secular"** to the Preamble, she redefined India's identity. Additionally, the introduction of **Fundamental Duties** shifted some responsibilities to the citizens, but critics argue that this was a distraction from the suppression of fundamental rights.

By manipulating the Constitution, Indira Gandhi transformed the democratic framework into a tool for authoritarian control. The Emergency exposed how fragile the Constitution could become when those in power are determined to exploit it for personal gain. While these changes were reversed after the Emergency through the **44th Amendment** in 1978, the scars of this period remain a potent reminder of how quickly a democracy can be subverted by constitutional manipulation.

The Fall of Indira Gandhi

When the elections were held, the people of India delivered a crushing verdict. Indira Gandhi and her Congress party were swept out of power in a humiliating defeat, and for the first time, a non-Congress government took control of the country. The Emergency officially ended, but the scars it left on the country's democratic fabric would never fully heal.

Solutions according to Varad Tikam

India's darkest chapter during the 1975 Emergency was a wake-up call. It exposed how fragile even the world's largest democracy could be when constitutional powers are manipulated. Indira Gandhi's actions during this period nearly turned the country into an autocracy, eroding the very rights that the Indian Constitution was built to protect. If there is one lesson we must learn from that era, it is that we need stronger constitutional safeguards to ensure that no government, regardless of the circumstances, can suppress the fundamental rights of its citizens or undermine the judicial system.

To protect our democracy from ever falling into such peril again, a series of legal and constitutional reforms are necessary. These changes would act as a shield, preventing the concentration of unchecked power in the hands of any leader, preserving the sanctity of fundamental rights, and ensuring that the judiciary retains its vital role as the guardian of the Constitution. Let's delve into these proposed reforms that will fortify India's democracy against any future attempts at dictatorship.

1. Absolute Protection of Fundamental Rights

The most egregious violation during the Emergency was the suspension of **fundamental rights**. The right to life, personal liberty, freedom of speech, and the right to move the courts were all ruthlessly stripped away. Citizens were left powerless as their rights were revoked overnight, turning India into a virtual police state.

To ensure this never happens again, we must amend the Constitution to explicitly state that **fundamental rights cannot be suspended under any circumstance.** Whether the nation is facing war, internal disturbances, or a declared Emergency, the basic rights of citizens must remain untouchable. This would guarantee that the government cannot silence dissent, arbitrarily detain its citizens, or impose censorship in the name of maintaining order. Fundamental rights are the very heart of the Indian Constitution, and they must remain intact, even in the most difficult times.

One of the most critical amendments required is a change to **Article 352**, which outlines the conditions for declaring an Emergency. This article must be revised to clarify that, even during an Emergency, the suspension of fundamental rights is unconstitutional. By protecting these rights, we safeguard the freedom and dignity of every Indian citizen, ensuring that no government can infringe upon their liberties.

2. The Judiciary as a Pillar of Democracy:

The Emergency of 1975 was a time when the judiciary was systematically weakened. Indira Gandhi's government passed amendments that severely limited the power of the courts, making it nearly impossible for them to challenge the executive's unconstitutional actions. The judiciary, which should have been a bulwark against such overreach, was rendered ineffective, and the checks and balances that define a healthy democracy were shattered.

To prevent this from happening again, we must restore and strengthen the judiciary's role through the full reinstatement of **judicial review**. Judicial review is the power of the courts to assess the constitutionality of the government's actions, laws, and policies. No law, no matter how powerful the government that enacts it, should be immune from judicial scrutiny. This ensures that every action taken by the executive and legislative branches can be checked by the judiciary to ensure it aligns with the principles of the Constitution.

A crucial safeguard must be the introduction of **automatic judicial review** for any declaration of Emergency. The Supreme Court should have the power to review and revoke an Emergency if it is found to be unjustified. This will prevent any government from using Emergency powers as a tool to suppress opposition or consolidate power. Furthermore, the controversial **Ninth Schedule**, which was used to shield laws from judicial scrutiny during the Emergency, should be strictly regulated or abolished to prevent future misuse.

The judiciary's role must be protected, not diminished. It is the pillar of democracy that ensures no leader or government is above the law.

3. Holding the Highest Offices Accountable

During the Emergency, the **39th Constitutional Amendment** shielded the highest offices in the country from judicial oversight, effectively placing the Prime Minister, President, Vice President, and Speaker beyond the reach of the law. This kind of immunity creates a dangerous precedent, allowing those in power to operate without fear of accountability, even if their actions are unconstitutional.

To safeguard democracy, we must ensure that **no office—no matter how high—remains immune from legal action**. The judiciary must have the power to hold even the Prime Minister and President accountable if they break the law or violate constitutional provisions. This includes the power to **arrest** and **prosecute** these officials if necessary.

A reversal of the **39th Amendment** is vital. No individual, regardless of their position, should be shielded from judicial scrutiny. If the head of state or government violates the Constitution or engages in corruption or electoral malpractice, they must be held accountable by the courts. This is not just a matter of justice but a fundamental principle of democracy: no one is above the law.

4. Limiting Executive Power During Emergencies

The Emergency allowed Indira Gandhi to centralize power to an unprecedented degree. The executive branch, led by the Prime Minister, gained immense authority, while the state governments and Parliament were sidelined. This concentration of power led to the widespread abuse of Emergency provisions, as the executive was free to arrest opposition leaders, censor the press, and suppress public dissent without any meaningful checks.

To prevent such abuses in the future, the Constitution must limit the **executive's power during Emergencies**. Any declaration of Emergency must be accompanied by a clear system of **checks and balances**, where both the Parliament and judiciary are actively involved in overseeing the actions of the executive.

Parliamentary oversight must be made mandatory during Emergencies, with regular reviews to ensure that Emergency powers are being used appropriately. Additionally, a special judicial review panel, independent of government influence, should be tasked with reviewing and, if necessary, curtailing the executive's powers during times of crisis. This ensures that no single branch of government can dominate the others, preserving the democratic structure.

5. Strengthening the Right to Constitutional Remedies

The most insidious part of the Emergency was the suspension of **constitutional remedies** under **Article 32**, which is the right to approach the Supreme Court directly when fundamental rights are violated. Without this safeguard, citizens had no recourse to challenge the government's arbitrary actions, leading to widespread detentions and abuses.

A vital reform would be to strengthen **Article 32**, ensuring that **courts remain accessible to all citizens, even during an Emergency**. This would prevent any future government from denying citizens their right to seek legal protection when their rights are violated. Courts must be empowered to immediately intervene in cases of unlawful detention, censorship, or any violation of rights, without delay.

In addition, we must ensure that the **Right to Constitutional Remedies** is clearly stated as inviolable under any circumstance. Even during times of war or internal unrest, the courts must remain open to protect citizens from the overreach of executive power.

6. *Regular Constitutional Review of Emergency Provisions*

To ensure that Emergency provisions are not abused again in the future, the Constitution should mandate a **regular review** of these provisions. Every five years, an independent body consisting of constitutional experts, legal scholars, and civil society representatives should assess whether the Emergency powers are being used in accordance with democratic principles.

This review would allow for necessary adjustments, ensuring that Emergency powers are only invoked in genuine crises and not as a tool for political gain. Regular constitutional review will act as a safeguard against authoritarian tendencies and preserve the democratic integrity of the nation.

Conclusion

The Emergency of 1975 exposed the vulnerabilities of India's democratic system, but it also taught us valuable lessons. The unchecked power of the executive, the suspension of fundamental rights, and the weakening of the judiciary allowed one leader to nearly turn India into a dictatorship. However, by introducing these constitutional safeguards, we can ensure that such an assault on democracy never happens again.

By **protecting fundamental rights, empowering the judiciary, holding leaders accountable, and limiting executive powers during crises**, we create a system where the balance of power is maintained, and no government can overstep its bounds. Democracy is a delicate system, but with these reforms, it can be fortified against any future attempts at dictatorship.

"Let us remember that the strength of a nation lies in its commitment to justice, freedom, and the rule of law, principles that no leader can be allowed to violate."

CHAPTER SEVEN

THE UNIVERSAL CARD

Introduction

The Universal Card represents a revolutionary step towards streamlining identification and service access in India. By integrating essential documents and personal data into one secure, multi-functional card, it aims to simplify everyday processes, enhance public safety, and improve the delivery of government services. From healthcare to financial transactions, the Universal Card offers a seamless solution, making life more efficient and secure for millions of citizens. This innovation not only addresses current challenges but also paves the way for a more connected and digitally empowered future.

The Vision

The Universal Card is envisioned as a single, comprehensive identification and data repository for Indian citizens, integrating and replacing existing identification and documentation systems such as Aadhaar card, PAN card, driving license, voter ID, and various other government-issued cards. This Universal Card aims to centralize and streamline access to a wide range of personal information, enhancing efficiency and security for both citizens and government authorities.

Key Features

The Universal Card is designed to streamline and simplify various aspects of daily life by consolidating key documents and providing access to comprehensive personal information in one secure platform. This consolidation addresses issues such as document loss, fraud, and inefficiency, making it a crucial tool for modernizing India's identification and service systems.

Consolidation of Documents

At its core, the Universal Card integrates multiple essential documents, including the Aadhaar card, PAN card, driving license, voter ID, and other relevant identity proofs. This consolidation eliminates the need for individuals to carry multiple physical cards, reducing the risk of loss and fraud. The single card simplifies identification processes, enabling individuals to access services without the hassle of managing various documents. Whether it's voting in elections or conducting financial transactions, the Universal Card becomes the key identifier.

Comprehensive Personal Data

Beyond just identity, the Universal Card stores extensive personal information. It includes vital details such as birth information, education history, bank account details, and medical records. On top of that, biometric data like fingerprints and iris scans are securely embedded within the system, ensuring that individuals can authenticate their identity with a high degree of security. This comprehensive database allows the card to function as a go-to resource for accessing critical personal information whenever required.

Unique QR Code and NFC Code

To ensure the ease of use, each Universal Card is equipped with a unique QR code and an NFC chip. This advanced technology enables the user to access stored information quickly, either by scanning the QR code or tapping the card on an NFC-enabled device. Whether at a healthcare facility, during financial transactions, or in everyday situations requiring verification, this feature guarantees both speed and accuracy, making interactions smoother and more efficient.

Medical Information

One of the most important features of the Universal Card is its ability to store detailed medical information. For healthcare providers, this allows instant access to a patient's medical history, ensuring more accurate diagnoses and timely treatment. Furthermore, family medical history can be included, which assists doctors in making more informed decisions regarding potential genetic or hereditary conditions. This not only improves patient care but also enhances long-term health management.

Law Enforcement Assistance

In the realm of public safety, the Universal Card proves invaluable. Law enforcement authorities can use the card to quickly and accurately identify individuals, whether it's for tracking down missing persons or identifying suspects. The ability to instantly access personal information boosts investigative efficiency, enhancing security and aiding in the swift resolution of cases.

Financial Transactions

The Universal Card also streamlines financial processes. With integrated bank account details, individuals can use the card for seamless financial transactions, including e-KYC procedures required by banks. By simplifying banking protocols, the card promotes financial inclusion, enabling more citizens to access banking services easily, and participate fully in the formal economy.

Education and Employment

Academic records and professional qualifications are securely stored on the Universal Card, offering a streamlined process for verifying credentials. For employers, this allows for a quick and reliable way to check an individual's qualifications, supporting a robust employment history record. In the long run, it enhances transparency and makes hiring more efficient by reducing the paperwork typically required in verifying an individual's educational and employment background.

Travel and Immigration

The Universal Card simplifies travel, serving as a valid identification for both domestic and international travel. For immigration purposes, the card can store visa details and travel history, streamlining the processes at checkpoints and minimizing delays. By making travel smoother, it facilitates international mobility for citizens, while also providing immigration authorities with the information needed to maintain security.

Government Services

Another advantage of the Universal Card is the ease with which individuals can access government services and benefits. The card ensures accurate identification when distributing subsidies or enrolling in welfare programs, reducing bureaucratic hurdles and ensuring timely service delivery. By minimizing fraud and errors, the Universal Card can improve the efficiency and fairness of government schemes.

Emergency Services

In emergency situations, the Universal Card proves critical. First responders can quickly access important emergency contacts and medical information, such as allergies or chronic conditions, improving the accuracy and speed of the response. This feature ensures that individuals receive the right care in times of crisis, potentially saving lives by reducing delays in medical attention.

In essence, the Universal Card offers a transformative solution for modernizing personal identification and service access across various sectors. By consolidating essential documents and providing a secure, comprehensive database of personal information, it enhances convenience, safety, and efficiency for both individuals and institutions.

Benefits

Imagine a world where you only need one card to manage your entire life. The Universal Card makes this possible by replacing the need for multiple documents. It simplifies everyday tasks, making things like identification and transactions much easier. Instead of carrying several cards or papers, you just carry one, reducing the risk of losing them or having them stolen.

Security is also a top priority. The Universal Card comes with advanced biometric features that protect your personal information, making it harder for anyone to steal your identity or commit fraud. Plus, all your data is stored safely in a central system, ensuring that only authorized people can access it.

The card also helps streamline government services. With everything integrated, you can access services faster and more accurately, cutting through the usual red tape and improving how government processes work. Healthcare is another area that benefits greatly. The card keeps a record of your entire medical history, which helps doctors provide better care. They'll be able to avoid medical errors and have a complete picture of your health whenever you need treatment.

For law enforcement, the Universal Card allows quick identification and verification. This helps keep the public safe and assists in solving criminal cases faster. In terms of economic growth, the card promotes financial inclusion by making it easier for people to open bank accounts and access financial services. It also simplifies tax processes, ensuring better compliance and contributing to the nation's economy.

Social welfare programs are more efficiently managed as well. The Universal Card ensures that benefits go directly to the right people, improving the system's accuracy. Additionally, when it comes to education and employment, the card helps verify qualifications quickly, creating a clear record of an individual's education and work history. Employers can easily check credentials, making hiring processes smoother and more reliable.

Implementation and Challenges

Implementing the Universal Card system would require a major overhaul of technology, infrastructure, and coordination across government and private sectors. Several challenges must be addressed to ensure the system's success, particularly around data security, interoperability, and public acceptance.

Data Privacy and Security

Protecting personal data will be one of the biggest concerns. The system needs to be highly secure against cyber threats like hacking or data breaches. This would require using advanced encryption methods, conducting regular security checks, and maintaining constant monitoring. Preventing unauthorized access is another key challenge, which would require strict controls on who can access sensitive information. Additionally, building public trust in the system will depend on showing transparency in how data is managed and secured.

Interoperability

The Universal Card system must integrate smoothly with the various databases and platforms that are already in use. Government departments, private businesses, and other entities will need to follow standardized protocols for data exchange to ensure compatibility. Moreover, data consistency will be crucial—any changes made in one system must automatically be reflected in others, maintaining accuracy across the board.

Infrastructure

Building the right technological infrastructure is essential. This includes setting up secure data centers, servers, and communication networks that can handle vast amounts of data and millions of daily transactions. Ensuring access in both urban and rural areas is equally important. Reliable internet connectivity across the country will prevent disparities and ensure that people everywhere can benefit from the Universal Card. Additionally, properly trained personnel will be needed to manage and operate the system effectively.

Regulatory and Legal Framework

Strong data protection laws will need to be crafted to address privacy concerns, data usage rights, and consent. These laws must safeguard citizens' information while still allowing for efficient use of data for public services. Ensuring the Universal Card complies with existing regulations and international standards will also be key, especially if there are any potential legal conflicts.

Cost and Resource Allocation

Implementing the system will require significant financial investment. Technology, infrastructure, staffing, and public awareness campaigns will all come at a cost. It will be important to identify sources of funding, such as government budgets, private investments, or international grants. Proper resource management will help ensure that the project is carried out efficiently without unnecessary spending.

Public Awareness and Acceptance

Getting people to adopt the Universal Card will involve extensive public outreach. Citizens need to understand how the card benefits them and be reassured about its security features. Addressing any concerns or myths will be crucial to building trust. Offering incentives for early adopters could help encourage acceptance, showing people firsthand how the system simplifies their daily lives.

Technical and Operational Challenges

To ensure everyone can use the system, it must have a user-friendly interface that works for all citizens, including those with disabilities or limited digital skills. Data migration will also be a challenge—moving information from existing systems into the new platform must be done carefully to avoid errors or disruptions. Lastly, a strong support and maintenance framework will be essential for troubleshooting issues and keeping the system updated and running smoothly.

In summary, while the Universal Card system promises great benefits in terms of convenience and efficiency, implementing it will require addressing complex technical, legal, and social challenges to ensure its success.

Roadmap for Implementation

Implementing the Universal Card system requires a carefully planned, phased approach to ensure success and address potential challenges effectively. The following roadmap outlines how the Indian government could systematically roll out the program, tackling each stage in a logical sequence.

Phase 1: Planning and Framework Development

The first step is engaging all relevant stakeholders. A dedicated task force must be formed, including representatives from various government departments, private sector experts, and civil society organizations. This task force will spearhead the project, ensuring coordination across all sectors. To start, extensive consultations with key stakeholders are necessary. These discussions will help gather valuable input, address concerns, and build consensus on the goals of the Universal Card system and its implementation strategy.

Alongside these efforts, a solid legal and regulatory framework must be established. Drafting and enacting comprehensive data protection laws is crucial to safeguarding personal information and ensuring privacy. These laws will cover all aspects of data handling, from collection and storage to processing and sharing. Furthermore, clear guidelines and standards for data privacy, security, and interoperability should be established. Aligning these guidelines with international best practices will ensure that the system is both secure and efficient.

Once the regulatory groundwork is laid, the next step is to conduct a feasibility study. This study will assess the technical, financial, and operational aspects of the project, identifying potential risks and strategies for mitigating them. To further refine the system before nationwide implementation, pilot projects can be launched in select regions. These pilots will test the system's functionality, gather user feedback, and allow for any necessary adjustments to be made.

Phase 2: Infrastructure and Capacity Building

With the plan in place, the next phase focuses on building the required infrastructure and capacity. Developing a robust technological infrastructure is key. This includes setting up secure data centers, servers, and communication networks that are scalable and resilient enough to handle the demands of the Universal Card system. Connectivity is another critical factor, as both urban and rural areas need reliable internet access to ensure equal participation in the system.

Simultaneously, efforts must be made to train personnel involved in managing and operating the system. This includes government employees and other stakeholders who will be responsible for the smooth functioning of the platform. Alongside personnel training, educational materials should be developed to help end-users—everyday citizens—understand how to use the Universal Card system effectively. User education will be crucial in ensuring widespread adoption and minimizing issues.

In parallel, the actual design and development of the Universal Card system will take place. This involves incorporating advanced encryption and biometric authentication mechanisms to ensure that the system is secure and reliable. The integration of existing government databases and systems is equally important. This integration will ensure seamless data exchange and synchronization across various platforms, making the Universal Card a one-stop solution for identification and services.

Phase 3: Pilot Implementation and Evaluation

The next phase involves testing the system under real-world conditions. The Universal Card system will be rolled out in select regions, covering a diverse mix of urban and rural areas to ensure that it functions well in all types of environments. Throughout this pilot implementation, the government will monitor the system closely to identify any issues and gather feedback from users.

A nationwide public awareness campaign will accompany this rollout, educating citizens about the benefits and security features of the Universal

Card. This campaign will leverage various communication channels, including social media, traditional media, and community outreach, to ensure that the public understands the value of the system. Addressing public concerns and resistance is vital during this phase, and transparent communication will help build trust. Highlighting success stories from the pilot regions can further encourage adoption.

As feedback is collected from the pilot regions, the task force will evaluate the system's performance against predefined metrics. Surveys, focus groups, and direct feedback mechanisms will provide insights into user experiences and areas for improvement. Based on this feedback, necessary adjustments will be made to the system. This could include refining the user interface, addressing technical issues, and improving operational processes to ensure the system is ready for full-scale implementation.

By following this phased approach, the Indian government can systematically address the challenges associated with the Universal Card system, ensuring a successful and efficient rollout across the country.

Conclusion

In conclusion, the Universal Card is a transformative tool that holds the potential to greatly simplify and enhance daily life for individuals across India. By consolidating multiple identification documents, providing instant access to personal, medical, and financial information, and integrating with government services, the card promises improved efficiency, security, and accessibility. While its implementation will require significant planning and safeguards to protect data privacy, the long-term benefits—ranging from streamlined services to enhanced public safety—are undeniable. The Universal Card represents a bold step toward a more connected, efficient, and digitally empowered nation.

CHAPTER EIGHT

NEED FOR GENDER EQUALITY

In recent years, the discourse around gender equality has primarily focused on addressing the challenges faced by women, often overlooking the unique struggles that men encounter in various aspects of life. From legal and social biases to health disparities and societal expectations, men face a range of issues that are rarely acknowledged or addressed. In family law, men frequently encounter disadvantages, particularly in custody battles and divorce settlements, where traditional gender roles and assumptions about caregiving often lead to unfavorable outcomes. Beyond the legal realm, men also grapple with significant health challenges, including mental health issues that are exacerbated by societal pressures to conform to notions of stoicism and emotional restraint. Moreover, the pervasive influence of toxic masculinity and rigid gender roles places immense pressure on men to adhere to specific behaviors and career paths, limiting their opportunities for personal and professional growth. By shedding light on these often-overlooked issues, this chapter seeks to explore the multifaceted challenges men face and advocate for a more balanced approach to gender equality that recognizes and addresses the needs of all individuals.

Legal and Social Biases Against Men

Men often face significant legal and social biases, particularly in family law. For instance, in custody battles and divorce cases, there is a prevailing assumption that mothers are inherently more suitable caregivers, which frequently results in fathers losing custody of their children. This bias extends to divorce settlements where men may face disadvantageous rulings regarding alimony and property division. Moreover, false accusations of dowry harassment, domestic violence, and sexual assault can severely affect men's lives, leading to prolonged legal battles, social stigma, and psychological distress. These legal challenges are compounded by societal attitudes that often dismiss men's complaints as less credible or significant compared to women's.

Health Issues Affecting Men

Men's health issues, particularly mental health, are often overlooked. Societal expectations of stoicism and emotional strength discourage men from seeking help for mental health problems, contributing to higher rates of untreated depression, anxiety, and suicide among men. Additionally, men are more likely to work in hazardous occupations, which results in higher rates of workplace injuries and fatalities. This combination of physical and mental health challenges underscores the need for greater awareness and resources dedicated to men's health issues.

Educational and Employment Pressures

Traditional gender roles impose significant pressures on men to be the primary breadwinners, which can lead to stress, overwork, and limited involvement in family life. Men are also subjected to societal expectations to pursue certain fields of study or careers that are deemed suitable for their gender, thereby restricting their personal and professional choices. These pressures not only affect men's well-being but also limit their opportunities to explore diverse interests and career paths.

Violence and Abuse Against Men

While domestic violence and sexual abuse are often associated with women, men can also be victims. Male victims of domestic violence face significant stigma and a lack of supportive services, which makes it difficult for them to seek help. Similarly, sexual abuse of men and boys is underreported due to societal shame and inadequate resources for male survivors. Addressing these issues requires a shift in societal attitudes and the development of support systems that recognize and respond to male victims of violence and abuse.

Social Expectations and Toxic Masculinity

Cultural norms around masculinity can be harmful to men, promoting behaviors such as aggression, emotional suppression, and risk-taking. These norms, often referred to as toxic masculinity, can lead to detrimental outcomes for men's mental and physical health. Men who do not conform to traditional gender roles, or who engage in behaviors considered feminine, may face ridicule, discrimination, and social ostracism. Challenging these harmful norms is essential for promoting a healthier and more inclusive understanding of masculinity.

Legal Disparities and Discrimination

Men face several legal disparities, particularly in areas where protections are more readily available for women. For example, laws such as the Protection of Women from Domestic Violence Act primarily focus on female victims, leaving male victims with fewer resources. Additionally, men often receive harsher sentences for similar crimes compared to women, reflecting a bias within the criminal justice system that presumes men as perpetrators rather than victims. Legal reforms are necessary to ensure that laws are gender-neutral and provide equal protection and rights to all individuals.

Parental Rights and Responsibilities

Men often struggle to assert their parental rights, especially in cases of separation or divorce where custody is predominantly awarded to mothers. The limited provision for paternity leave in India reflects a broader societal expectation that childcare is primarily the mother's responsibility, hindering men's involvement in early child-rearing. Promoting policies that support men's roles as active and engaged fathers is crucial for achieving gender equality in parenting.

Solutions according to Varad Tikam

Constitutional Amendments for Legal and Social Biases Against Men

To enhance gender equality in India, constitutional amendments should focus on ensuring all language within the Constitution is gender-neutral, replacing references to "he" with inclusive terms such as "they" or explicitly stating "he or she." Additionally, introducing specific provisions to protect men's rights can address issues such as false accusations, domestic violence, and workplace harassment, ensuring a balanced approach to gender equality.

Legal Reforms

Legal reforms are crucial for addressing the current gaps in gender equality. Implementing a Uniform Civil Code (UCC) would replace religion-based personal laws with a common set of laws governing marriage, divorce, inheritance, and adoption, ensuring gender neutrality and equality across all communities. Family law reforms should include changes to custody laws, ensuring fathers have equal rights and opportunities in custody battles, promoting shared parenting. Furthermore, amending the Protection of Women from Domestic Violence Act to include protections for male victims would provide gender-neutral support services, ensuring all victims of domestic violence receive adequate protection. Expanding the definition of sexual harassment and abuse to be gender-neutral is essential to ensure that men and boys who are victims receive the same legal protections and support as women.

Policy and Administrative Changes

Policy and administrative changes should focus on creating comprehensive mental health services and awareness campaigns tailored to men's mental health issues, encouraging men to seek help and reducing the associated stigma. Implementing workplace policies that promote work-life balance for both men and women, such as mandatory paternity leave, flexible working hours, and workplace childcare facilities, would support a more equitable work environment. Strict enforcement of equal pay for equal work policies is necessary to eliminate the gender pay gap. Educational initiatives should introduce gender sensitivity training in schools and workplaces to challenge traditional gender roles and stereotypes, promoting equal opportunities in education and vocational training for all genders and ensuring that career choices are not limited by societal expectations.

Political and Social Changes

Increasing women's representation in all levels of government through reservations or other affirmative actions is essential until a balanced representation is achieved. Political parties should be encouraged to field more female candidates and support their campaigns to ensure a more gender-balanced political landscape. Nationwide awareness campaigns can promote gender equality, challenge stereotypes, and educate the public about the importance of gender-neutral laws and policies. Engaging men as allies in gender equality efforts is crucial, emphasizing the benefits of a more equitable society for everyone.

Strengthening Existing Provisions

Strengthening the mechanisms for enforcing existing gender equality laws is vital, ensuring that violations are promptly and effectively addressed. Enhancing the training of law enforcement and judiciary officials on gender sensitivity and the importance of unbiased law enforcement can improve the implementation of these laws. Judicial reforms should focus on expediting the judicial process for gender-related cases to ensure timely justice, reduce the backlog of cases, and prevent prolonged legal battles. Establishing specialized courts or tribunals to handle gender-related cases with expertise and sensitivity would further support the effective enforcement of gender equality laws.

Conclusion

Achieving true gender equality in India requires a multifaceted approach involving constitutional amendments, legal reforms, policy changes, and societal shifts. By ensuring gender-neutral language in the Constitution, protecting men's rights, implementing a Uniform Civil Code, and making comprehensive legal and policy changes, India can move closer to a society where all individuals, regardless of gender, have equal opportunities, rights, and protections. Enhanced enforcement mechanisms, judicial reforms, and nationwide awareness campaigns are also essential to address existing biases and promote a more inclusive and equitable society.

Bill To be Proposed

As I envision Bharat's rise to the status of Vishwaguru—a global leader that others look to for guidance and wisdom—I recognize that true leadership begins with justice and equality within our own borders. The *Equality and Justice Bill, 20XX* is a critical step in this direction. Through this Bill, I propose a transformative framework that addresses the deep-rooted legal and social biases that have long hindered our progress toward a truly inclusive society.

By implementing these comprehensive reforms, I believe we can build a nation where every individual, regardless of gender, has equal rights, opportunities, and protections. This isn't just about correcting past injustices; it's about laying the groundwork for a Bharat that leads the world by example, embodying the principles of fairness and compassion that we hold dear. For Bharat to truly become Vishwaguru, we must first ensure that our society stands as a beacon of equality and justice for all. This Bill is my commitment to that vision, and I am confident that its enactment will bring us closer to realizing our destiny as a global leader.

Equality and Justice Bill, 20XX

A BILL

To amend the Constitution of India and various laws to ensure comprehensive gender equality, addressing legal, social, economic, and political disparities, and to introduce new provisions and policies for the same.

Be it enacted by the Parliament of India as follows:

Part I: Preliminary

1. Short Title and Commencement

1. This Act may be called the Equality and Justice Act, 2024.
2. It shall come into force on such date as the Central Government may, by notification in the Official Gazette, appoint.

2. Definitions

1. In this Act, unless the context otherwise requires:

    - "Gender" includes male, female, transgender, and other gender identities (if any).
    - "Discrimination" means any distinction, exclusion, or restriction made on the basis of gender.
    - "Harassment" includes any unwelcome behavior of a sexual nature or any other conduct that affects the dignity of individuals, regardless of gender.

Part II: Constitutional Amendments
3. Amendment of the Constitution

1. The Constitution of India is hereby amended as follows:

    - **Article 14:** Insert "and gender" after "sex" in "The State shall not deny to any person equality before the law or the equal protection of the laws within the territory of India."
    - **Article 15:** Amend to read "The State shall not discriminate against any citizen on grounds only of religion, race, caste, sex, gender, place of birth or any of them."
    - **Article 21:** Ensure the right to life and personal liberty is upheld with gender-neutral language, including explicit protection for mental health and protection against false accusations.

Part III: Legal Reforms
4. Uniform Civil Code

1. The government shall constitute a committee to draft a Uniform Civil Code (UCC) that shall replace personal laws based on religion with a common set of laws governing marriage, divorce, inheritance, and adoption, ensuring gender neutrality and equality.

5. Custody and Divorce Laws

1. Amend the Hindu Marriage Act, 1955, and the Special Marriage Act, 1954, to ensure equal rights and opportunities for fathers in custody battles, promoting shared parenting.
2. Reform alimony and property division laws to remove gender biases and ensure equitable settlements.

6. Protection Against Domestic Violence

1. Amend the Protection of Women from Domestic Violence Act, 2005, to include protections for male victims and provide gender-neutral support services.

7. Sexual Harassment and Abuse

1. Amend the Sexual Harassment of Women at Workplace (Prevention, Prohibition and Redressal) Act, 2013, to be gender-neutral, extending protections to all genders.
2. Amend the Indian Penal Code to ensure that definitions of sexual harassment and abuse are gender-neutral.

8. Criminal Law Reforms

1. Amend the Indian Penal Code to introduce strict penalties for filing false accusations of crimes such as dowry harassment, domestic violence, and sexual assault.
2. Ensure that all allegations of gender-based crimes are investigated with impartiality and without bias.

9. Protection of Transgender Rights

1. Implement the Transgender Persons (Protection of Rights) Act, 2019, with additional provisions to ensure comprehensive protection and inclusion of transgender individuals in all aspects of society.

Part IV: Policy and Administrative Changes
10. Mental Health Services

1. The Ministry of Health and Family Welfare shall establish comprehensive mental health services and awareness campaigns tailored to men's mental health issues, encouraging men to seek help and reducing stigma.

11. Workplace Equality

1. Implement mandatory paternity leave policies, flexible working hours, and workplace childcare facilities.
2. Enforce strict equal pay for equal work policies to eliminate the gender pay gap.
3. Introduce policies to prevent workplace discrimination based on gender identity or expression.

12. Educational Initiatives

1. Introduce gender sensitivity training in schools and workplaces to challenge traditional gender roles and stereotypes.
2. Promote equal opportunities in education and vocational training for all genders, ensuring career choices are not limited by societal expectations.
3. Implement scholarships and incentives for women and transgender individuals in STEM fields to promote diversity in traditionally male-dominated industries.

13. Economic Empowerment

1. Create programs to support female and transgender entrepreneurs, including access to credit, training, and mentorship.
2. Encourage companies to implement diversity and inclusion policies, with incentives for those demonstrating significant progress.

Part V: Political and Social Changes
14. Political Representation

1. Introduce reservations or affirmative actions to increase women's representation in all levels of government until balanced representation is achieved.

2. Encourage political parties to field more female and transgender candidates and support their campaigns.

15. Awareness Campaigns

1. Launch nationwide awareness campaigns to promote gender equality, challenge stereotypes, and educate the public about the importance of gender-neutral laws and policies.
2. Engage men as allies in gender equality efforts, emphasizing the benefits of a more equitable society for everyone.

Part VI: Strengthening Existing Provisions
16. Enforcement Mechanisms

1. Strengthen the mechanisms for enforcing existing gender equality laws, ensuring violations are promptly and effectively addressed.
2. Enhance the training of law enforcement and judiciary officials on gender sensitivity and unbiased law enforcement.

17. Judicial Reforms

1. Expedite the judicial process for gender-related cases to ensure timely justice, reduce the backlog of cases, and prevent prolonged legal battles.
2. Establish specialized courts or tribunals to handle gender-related cases with expertise and sensitivity.

18. Monitoring and Accountability

1. Establish an independent commission to monitor the implementation of gender equality laws and policies.
2. Require annual reports on the progress of gender equality initiatives, with recommendations for further action.

Part VII: Funding and Implementation
19. Funding

1. Allocate appropriate funding from the central and state governments for the implementation of this Act.

2. Establish a monitoring body to oversee the effective utilization of funds and implementation of provisions.

20. Implementation

1. Set up a task force to ensure the coordinated implementation of all sections of this Act across different states and sectors.
2. Conduct regular reviews and assessments to measure the impact of the Act and make necessary adjustments.

Part VIII: Miscellaneous
21. Power to Make Rules

1. The Central Government may, by notification in the Official Gazette, make rules for carrying out the provisions of this Act.

22. Removal of Difficulties

1. If any difficulty arises in giving effect to the provisions of this Act, the Central Government may, by order published in the Official Gazette, make such provisions not inconsistent with the provisions of this Act as appear to it to be necessary or expedient for removing the difficulty.

Statement of Objects and Reasons

The Equality and Justice Bill, 20XX, seeks to address the multifaceted issues related to gender equality in India by amending the Constitution, reforming existing laws, and introducing new policies and initiatives. The Bill aims to create a society where all individuals, regardless of gender, have equal opportunities, rights, and protections. It underscores the need for comprehensive changes across legal, social, economic, and political domains to achieve true gender equality.

CHAPTER NINE

GAYS, LESBIANS, AND TRANS INDIVIDUALS

As I stand before the vision of an India that rises to become a global leader, *Vishwaguru*, I cannot help but reflect on the pressing issues that challenge our progress. Among these challenges is the marginalization and discrimination faced by members of the LGBTQ+ community, particularly gays, lesbians, and transgender individuals. In a country as rich in cultural heritage as ours, it is disheartening that we have failed to extend these individuals the same respect, dignity, and protection as we do to others. This issue is not just about human rights but about ensuring that India stands as a beacon of equality and justice, showing the world that we honor our traditions while embracing progressive ideals.

For India to truly lead on the world stage, it must address the inequalities still embedded in our social fabric. Legalizing and protecting the rights of gays, lesbians, and transgender individuals is a critical step toward achieving this goal. This aligns with our ancient texts and traditions, which have long recognized diverse sexual and gender identities. The urgent need for reforms in this area is not only about justice; it is about setting a new standard for human rights and inclusivity, which will propel India forward as a global role model

Historical and Cultural Context: LGBTQ+ Identities in Indian Epics

India's epics, the Ramayana and Mahabharata, are often regarded as foundational texts that shape much of our cultural and moral understanding. Interestingly, within these ancient scriptures, we find narratives that reflect a diversity of gender identities and relationships, reinforcing that such concepts are not new or foreign to our traditions. These stories offer insights into how diverse identities were acknowledged and respected in ancient India, providing a cultural basis for the acceptance of modern LGBTQ+ rights.

Transgender Identity in the Ramayana

One compelling example of transgender recognition comes from the Ramayana. When Lord Rama was exiled to the forest, he instructed the men and women of Ayodhya to return to their homes. However, a group of hijras (traditionally understood as individuals who identify outside the male-female binary) remained at the spot, refusing to leave. Upon his return 14 years later, Rama blessed them for their devotion, giving them the power to confer blessings on auspicious occasions such as childbirth and marriage.

This story reflects how transgender individuals, known as hijras, held a unique and respected role in ancient Indian society. Even today, hijras continue to be a significant part of Indian cultural and religious traditions, offering blessings during important life events. This narrative, embedded in one of India's most revered epics, shows that the concept of gender diversity has been a recognized and valued part of Indian culture for centuries.

Gender Fluidity and Same-Sex Relationships in the Mahabharata

In the Mahabharata, the story of Shikhandi is a significant example of gender fluidity. Born as Shikhandini, the daughter of King Drupada, Shikhandini was raised as a woman but later transitioned to male, taking on the name Shikhandi. This transformation was accepted, and Shikhandi eventually married a woman, reflecting a form of gender identity that does not strictly conform to the binary male-female understanding. While not explicitly about lesbianism in the modern sense, this narrative has been interpreted by some scholars as a reflection of the acceptance of diverse gender roles and relationships in ancient India.

Shikhandi played a crucial role in the Mahabharata, particularly in the battle of Kurukshetra. As a warrior, Shikhandi was instrumental in the defeat of Bhishma, one of the most powerful figures on the battlefield. This story symbolizes how ancient Indian society acknowledged the complexities of gender and honored individuals based on their contributions, irrespective of their gender identity.

This narrative offers a culturally rooted understanding of gender fluidity and shows how ancient texts like the Mahabharata included space for non-binary and diverse identities. Such stories can serve as a bridge between traditional Indian values and the progressive movement toward LGBTQ+ rights in modern India.

Sources:

'19 LGBT Hindu Gods'', by Jacob Ogles, September 06, 2016, 6:23 AM EST (www.advocate.com)

The Problem

Although Section 377 was partially repealed in 2018, making homosexuality legal, the LGBTQ+ community still struggles with discrimination across various sectors, including employment, education, and healthcare. The law may have changed, but societal attitudes remain rigid. According to a 2021 survey by the Human Rights Campaign, over 70% of LGBTQ+ individuals in India still reported facing discrimination in their daily lives.

The problem becomes more severe when we consider healthcare. Many LGBT people avoid seeking medical help due to fear of prejudice. Healthcare professionals are often not sensitized to the unique challenges faced by this community, leading to inadequate or outright discriminatory treatment. Similarly, in the workplace, many LGBT individuals feel compelled to hide their identities, fearing harassment or job loss.

One of the most prominent real-life examples of this discrimination can be found in the story of a transgender woman from Chennai, who faced extreme hardship finding a job despite her qualifications. She was rejected from over 50 companies simply because of her gender identity. Stories like this are far too common in India, demonstrating that while the legal battle may have been won, the social struggle is far from over.

According to Varad Tikam,

Legalizing Same-Sex Marriage

One of the most impactful ways to ensure equality for LGBT individuals is through the legalization of same-sex marriage. Recognizing same-sex marriages legally is not just a matter of granting formal status to these relationships; it's about affirming the rights and dignity of LGBT individuals and ensuring they have the same legal protections as heterosexual couples.

Conclusion

In closing, I want to reaffirm my stance on this crucial issue. While I firmly support the rights and dignity of individuals across all sexual orientations, my position on gender identity is more nuanced. I advocate for respect and equality for all sexual orientations, understanding that everyone should be free to love who they choose without fear of discrimination.

However, my perspective on gender identity remains aligned with traditional views on sex assigned at birth. I recognize that this viewpoint might differ from the broader discussions on gender fluidity and non-binary identities, but it is important to clarify where I stand on these matters.

By focusing on sexual orientations, we can work together to build a society where everyone is treated with respect and has equal opportunities, while also engaging in open and respectful dialogues about gender identity and its complexities. Let us move forward with compassion and understanding, ensuring that our efforts toward inclusivity and equality reflect our commitment to the fundamental rights of all individuals.

CHAPTER TEN

AGNIPATH SCHEME

The Agnipath Scheme, launched by the Indian government, proposes a new model of recruitment into the Indian Armed Forces. According to the plan, young recruits—called "Agniveers"—would serve for a period of four years, after which only a select few would be retained for permanent roles. On the surface, the scheme appears to be an innovative approach to modernizing the military and cutting down on defense expenditures. However, I firmly believe this scheme is not the right step for India's defense forces, and here's why.

The military of any country is its backbone, representing both its strength and its readiness in times of crisis. Recruitment into the defense forces should not be treated like a temporary employment opportunity. The short-term nature of the Agnipath scheme threatens the long-term stability and effectiveness of India's military. Defense forces are built on experience, discipline, and a deep-rooted understanding of warfare—things that cannot be fully cultivated in just four years.

Problems

Lack of Experience

One of the primary reasons I oppose this scheme is the sheer lack of experience that short-term recruits would bring to the table. The Agnipath scheme envisions soldiers being trained and deployed for only four years, after which the majority would leave the forces. However, it takes years—sometimes decades—for military personnel to become proficient in their roles, especially in specialized areas such as intelligence, strategy, or high-tech warfare. By keeping soldiers in service for only four years, we are essentially depriving the military of seasoned individuals who can contribute not just in the field but also in terms of strategy, leadership, and decision-making.

A soldier's first few years are generally dedicated to rigorous training and on-the-ground learning. After their initial training, they develop the real skills necessary to handle complex military operations. Under the Agnipath scheme, just as soldiers are gaining valuable experience, they are expected to leave the forces. This turnover will likely lead to a deficit of experienced soldiers, leaving the military reliant on a constantly rotating workforce of relatively inexperienced personnel.

Compromising National Security

National security is not something we can afford to compromise, even in the slightest. With the constant threat of border tensions, terrorism, and insurgency, India needs a stable and experienced military. The Agnipath scheme risks turning the Indian military into a revolving door of temporary recruits. These short-term soldiers, once discharged, may struggle to find opportunities in the civilian world, potentially leaving them disillusioned and vulnerable to negative influences. Moreover, there is the added risk of sensitive military knowledge being unintentionally leaked or misused once these soldiers are back in civilian life.

Our borders, especially with Pakistan and China, require round-the-clock vigilance and a robust military presence. Can we really depend on a short-term force to guard our nation in such volatile areas? A temporary workforce lacks the long-term dedication, attachment, and motivation required to serve and defend with the intensity that permanent soldiers bring.

Disrupting Military Culture

The military is not just an institution; it is a culture—a way of life built on principles of discipline, loyalty, and brotherhood. Short-term schemes like Agnipath risk disrupting this culture. The military is not just about physical fitness or technical skills; it's about creating bonds that last a lifetime. When you know that your fellow soldier is here to stay, you are more likely to develop that sense of camaraderie, trust, and shared responsibility that is crucial in life-or-death situations. The short-term nature of the Agnipath scheme undermines this essential aspect of military life.

Moreover, military discipline is not something that can be instilled quickly or temporarily. It requires a deep-rooted sense of belonging and commitment to the cause. Under the Agnipath scheme, soldiers might not develop that level of attachment to the uniform or the institution, knowing their stint is temporary.

Alternatives to Agnipath

Economic Concerns and the Future of Ex-Servicemen

Another concern is the future of the Agniveers after their four years of service. While the government promises various schemes to ensure that these recruits are absorbed into civilian jobs, the reality might be much harsher. After spending four years in a highly regimented and specialized environment, many may struggle to transition into civilian roles. There is also a danger that without proper rehabilitation and reintegration programs, ex-Agniveers could find themselves disillusioned and unemployed, leading to social unrest.

The Agnipath scheme may save the government money in the short term by cutting pension and salary costs, but at what cost? By not providing long-term careers in the military, we are effectively removing one of the primary motivators for young people to join the armed forces. The promise of a secure future—both in terms of employment and financial stability—has always been a key incentive for recruitment. Removing this assurance might lead to a decrease in the quality of recruits, as many talented individuals may be deterred from joining the military for only a four-year period.

While the Indian government's Agnipath Scheme aims to address budget constraints and modernize recruitment, it presents significant risks to the stability, experience, and discipline of India's military. Several countries across the world have developed models that offer long-term stability while managing costs and maintaining the dignity of their armed forces. These models can serve as valuable alternatives for India's defense strategy without compromising the strength, integrity, or professionalism of its military.

1. United States: The Reserve Component Model

The U.S. military operates a highly effective **Reserve Component Model**, consisting of the National Guard and Reserves. These units consist of trained soldiers who serve part-time, allowing them to hold civilian jobs while maintaining military readiness. Members of the reserves are called up for active duty during national emergencies, conflicts, or natural disasters.

This model allows the U.S. to maintain a large pool of trained, experienced personnel who are not full-time soldiers but can be mobilized when needed. India could adopt a similar approach by expanding its own reserve forces, where trained individuals continue their careers in civilian life but remain available for service in times of need. This offers the following advantages:

- **Cost Efficiency**: The military only needs to pay full-time salaries for active-duty personnel, while reservists are compensated when mobilized or during periodic training.
- **Retaining Experience**: Soldiers remain connected to the military throughout their careers, ensuring long-term engagement with defense needs.
- **Dignity in Service**: Soldiers continue to hold military rank and are treated as valued members of the forces, preserving their honor and identity.

By using this reserve model, India could ensure a steady supply of trained soldiers without the risks of short-term recruits.

2. *Israel: Mandatory Conscription with Long-Term Engagement*

Israel operates a **mandatory conscription** system for all citizens, with men serving for three years and women for two. What makes Israel's system particularly valuable as a model is its **post-service commitment**, where conscripts remain in the reserve forces for many years after their initial service. They undergo periodic training and can be called upon in times of conflict or national security crises.

This system not only ensures that a large portion of the population is militarily trained but also maintains a sense of duty and responsibility long after active service ends. For India, adopting a similar model could mean:

- **Conscription with Extended Service**: All recruits serve for a longer, mandatory period of 3-4 years, but after their initial service, they become part of the reserve, ensuring continued engagement and readiness.
- **National Defense Readiness**: The system creates a military-ready population that can be called upon in times of war or emergency.
- **Civic Responsibility**: Mandatory service fosters a deep sense of patriotism and civic duty while maintaining the dignity and value of long-term military participation.

Israel's conscription model is widely respected and could serve as a strong alternative to short-term contracts like Agnipath.

3. *Switzerland: Citizen-Soldier Model*

Switzerland's **citizen-soldier model** is another effective system that India could learn from. Swiss males are required to undergo basic military training for a few months, after which they are placed in the reserve forces. Swiss soldiers are expected to keep their gear at home and remain ready to serve the country whenever needed, even while leading civilian lives.

This system is unique in that it combines the benefits of both a professional military and a highly trained civilian population. India could consider adopting similar features, such as:

- **Periodic Refresher Training**: Swiss reservists undergo regular refresher courses, which ensures that their skills are up-to-date even as they lead civilian lives. This would ensure India's soldiers remain combat-ready while serving their civilian careers.
- **Maintaining Dignity of Service**: The model allows citizens to fulfill both military and civilian duties with pride, ensuring that soldiers are always treated with the respect they deserve.
- **Integration into Society**: Soldiers remain integrated into civilian life while staying ready for national defense, creating a seamless connection between military readiness and civilian engagement.

Adopting a Swiss-style citizen-soldier model would allow India to create a large pool of trained reservists without sacrificing military professionalism or dignity.

4. *United Kingdom: Territorial Army Model*

The **United Kingdom's Territorial Army (now called the Army Reserve)** provides a strong example of how countries can effectively utilize part-time soldiers without undermining the long-term stability of their armed forces. The Territorial Army consists of individuals who serve part-time, typically holding civilian jobs, but who receive military training and can be deployed alongside regular forces during emergencies or conflicts.

India could consider expanding its existing territorial forces and adopting the following features of the UK model:

- **Training and Deployment Flexibility**: Territorial soldiers undergo training during weekends and for short periods throughout the year, making it easy for them to balance military service with civilian life. This could appeal to young Indians who want to serve their country but also wish to pursue other career opportunities.
- **Enhanced Retention**: Soldiers remain connected to the military over a longer period, ensuring that their experience and skills are not lost.
- **Dignified Role**: Territorial Army members are considered integral to the national defense strategy, ensuring they are honored for their service, rather than seen as temporary or expendable.

This model provides the perfect blend of part-time military service and long-term national defense readiness, ensuring soldiers remain a vital part of India's defense strategy without the drawbacks of short-term contracts.

5. France: Foreign Legion Model

The **French Foreign Legion** provides a unique model that blends recruitment from foreign nationals with long-term service opportunities. While the Indian context may not directly align with recruiting foreign nationals, the **long-term enlistment** and **specialized units** that the French Foreign Legion operates can provide useful insights for India.

In the Foreign Legion, soldiers are recruited for an initial five-year contract, with opportunities to extend their service. This model is focused on creating elite units with specialized training. India could adapt this by:

- **Creating Elite, Specialized Units**: Instead of focusing on short-term soldiers, India could recruit for longer-term elite units with specialized training in areas such as counter-terrorism, cyber defense, and mountain warfare. These units would require a higher commitment and offer more training and incentives.
- **Extended Contracts**: Instead of a four-year stint, soldiers could be recruited for longer, more dignified contracts (6–8 years) with benefits tied to their service, ensuring that they remain committed and that the military retains its professionalism.

By focusing on creating elite, long-term units, India could maintain the dignity of its armed forces and ensure the continuous development of specialized, highly trained soldiers.

Conclusion

As India contemplates military reforms, it is essential to learn from countries that have effectively managed the balance between cost-saving measures and maintaining a dignified, professional, and experienced defense force. The Agnipath Scheme, while well-intentioned, risks undermining the values and long-term stability that are essential to India's armed forces.

By adopting models like the **U.S. Reserve Component, Israel's mandatory conscription**, Switzerland's **citizen-soldier system**, the UK's **Territorial Army**, and France's **Foreign Legion**, India can create a robust, modern defense force while ensuring the dignity and professionalism of military service remains intact. These alternatives provide a clear path for strengthening India's military without resorting to short-term, high-risk solutions that may weaken the defense forces in the long run.

CHAPTER ELEVEN

NOTA

As I sit to reflect on the current state of Indian democracy, one thought consistently haunts me: Are we truly giving the power to the people? Elections, the very foundation of our democracy, should be an opportunity for the citizens to voice their opinions and choose their leaders, but more often than not, we are left choosing between bad options. The electorate, in many cases, feels cornered—voting for a candidate, not out of preference but as the lesser evil. This is where the NOTA (None of the Above) button should ideally come in as a voice for the disillusioned voters. However, NOTA, in its current form, lacks the power to force change.

As we envision India as Vishwaguru, a global leader, we must ensure that our democracy functions at its highest potential. Our political system should reflect the aspirations of the people. The NOTA button is a symbol of their dissatisfaction, but it needs to be more than that—it must lead to tangible outcomes. For this, we need to reform the election system so that NOTA holds real value and becomes an instrument of accountability, one that reshapes our democratic processes.

The Problem of Symbolic NOTA and Unaccountable Candidates:

Currently, the NOTA button serves only as a symbolic protest vote. It allows voters to reject all candidates in a given election, but it does nothing to change the actual outcome. Even if a large percentage of the electorate chooses NOTA, the candidate with the most votes still wins, irrespective of whether they have the majority mandate or not. Let me paint a scenario to illustrate the problem.

Imagine a constituency where 100,000 voters cast their ballots. Candidate A gets 25,000 votes, Candidate B gets 20,000, and Candidate C gets 15,000 votes. Meanwhile, NOTA receives 40,000 votes—more than any individual candidate. Despite NOTA receiving the most votes, Candidate A still wins, because, under the current system, the vote for NOTA does not impact the results. This outcome blatantly disregards the will of the majority, who have clearly expressed their dissatisfaction with all the candidates. Is this real democracy? Clearly not.

This symbolic nature of NOTA reduces its value and does nothing to encourage better candidates. The current system allows political parties to recycle unfit candidates, knowing that voters have no real alternative but to select the "least bad" option. This is not the democracy envisioned by our forefathers.

Solutions according to Varad Tikam

Ban Candidates Scoring Less than NOTA from Contesting for 6 Years

One of the core reforms I propose is that any candidate who receives fewer votes than the NOTA option should be barred from contesting elections for a period of six years. This measure would ensure that political parties are more cautious about the candidates they put forward. No longer would they be able to field individuals with a tarnished reputation, criminal records, or poor performance in previous terms.

The people of India deserve better, and by giving NOTA the power to disqualify such candidates, we raise the standard of politics. Consider a real-world example of the 2022 Bihar Assembly elections, where nearly 6% of the voters chose NOTA, more than the vote share of some winning candidates. Under my proposal, those candidates who failed to gain more votes than NOTA would be banned for six years, forcing political parties to choose candidates who are truly capable and ethical.

Re-Elections with New Candidates if NOTA Secures Majority

If NOTA wins the majority in any constituency, it should automatically trigger re-elections. The voters have spoken loud and clear—they do not want any of the available candidates. In such cases, re-elections must be held, and all the previous candidates should be banned from contesting again. Furthermore, new candidates should not be allowed to have any close ties with the previous candidates, including family members, friends, or business partners.

Take, for example, the 2019 Haryana Assembly elections, where in several constituencies, NOTA polled higher than certain political parties. Had NOTA carried the weight it deserves, it would have triggered re-elections with new, unrelated candidates, giving the electorate a fresh slate. This would prevent political dynasties from continuing to dominate, ensuring that voters are given genuinely new choices.

In a country as large and diverse as India, it is essential that our democracy reflects this diversity. By mandating re-elections with new candidates when NOTA wins the majority, we ensure that the people's voice is respected. This would also curb nepotism in politics, ensuring that only those with merit, not familial or financial connections, get to represent the people.

Incentivizing Political Parties to Improve Candidate Selection

Another important reform to strengthen the role of NOTA is to create incentives for political parties to improve their candidate selection process. If NOTA is empowered as proposed, parties will have to rethink how they choose their candidates. Political parties could be penalized for fielding candidates who perform worse than NOTA, including a reduction in party funding or a temporary suspension of their registration in the given constituency.

In a scenario where NOTA receives significant support, it would send a message to political parties that their candidate selection processes need to improve. Parties will have to ensure that candidates are not only competent but also resonate with the electorate's aspirations. This reform would force political parties to evolve and become more democratic in their internal processes.

Publicly Funded Voter Education Campaigns

Another key reform involves educating voters on the importance of NOTA and how its empowerment can shape political accountability. Publicly funded voter education campaigns can raise awareness about the implications of voting NOTA and encourage citizens to use it when dissatisfied with their options. A study by the Lokniti-CSDS in 2020 found that many voters are unaware of the role of NOTA or mistakenly believe it has a decisive impact when in reality, it does not.

By empowering voters with knowledge, they can become more active participants in the democratic process. This will encourage parties to field candidates that resonate with the electorate, as an informed voter base will be more likely to use NOTA strategically.

Conclusion:

As I reflect on the journey ahead, it becomes clear that empowering NOTA is not merely about improving the electoral system—it is about restoring the faith of the people in democracy. Our current system, which allows unworthy candidates to win despite widespread dissatisfaction, must evolve. By empowering the NOTA button, we hold our political class accountable to the people they seek to represent.

The power to reject unsuitable candidates and force a re-election with new faces can transform the Indian political landscape. With better candidates, political parties will have no choice but to field individuals who truly reflect the values and aspirations of the people. This change will foster a stronger democracy, where leaders emerge based on merit, integrity, and competence.

In our quest to make Bharat Vishwaguru, we cannot ignore the importance of building a clean, accountable political system. Empowering

NOTA is a crucial step toward achieving that goal. It is a reform that honors the voice of the people, ensuring that their vote always matters, even when they choose "None of the Above." Together, we can create a democracy that truly reflects the will of the people and builds the future we envision for India—a global leader in every sense of the word.

> "*Empowering NOTA is the key to revolutionizing our democracy, giving the power back to the people and paving the way for a stronger, brighter India.*"

CHAPTER TWELVE

REALITY OF WOMEN'S RESERVATION BILL IN INDIA

The Indian government has passed the historic Women's Reservation Bill, which mandates that 33% of seats in the Lok Sabha and state assemblies will be reserved for women. This development has sparked significant interest, as every political party seems eager to take credit for the bill.

Currently, women make up 15% of MPs in the Lok Sabha and 13% in the Rajya Sabha, which is lower compared to other countries, including Bangladesh. This has led to expressions of gratitude from many female MPs towards the Prime Minister. However, there is also concern among the public. The primary aim of the bill is to enhance women's representation in Indian politics. Yet, it is often observed that women contesting elections may not always be independent candidates but rather the wives or daughters of politicians.

For instance, an incident in Ballia district, Uttar Pradesh, in 2021 highlights this issue, where a 45-year-old woman, Hathi Singh, who had vowed to remain celibate for life, had been trying to become a Sarpanch for 10 years. In 2015, he narrowly lost the election by 57 votes, finishing in second place. He was hopeful about winning the next election, but the seat was reserved for women. His mother, who was very old, did not trust any other woman to take on the role. Frustrated by the situation, Hathi Singh decided to marry and make his wife the head of the panchayat.

The question arises whether what happened with Hathi Singh in UP might occur across the country with the implementation of the Women's

Reservation Bill. Fortunately, numerous research papers have been published to explore this very issue. However, to fully grasp the implications, it is essential to understand the history of this bill.

History of this bill

The discussion surrounding the Women's Reservation Bill did not begin this year; it started back in 1996. It took over 25 years for the bill to finally gain approval. During this period, prominent leaders such as Lalu Pr***d Y*d*v and Yogi Adity***th voiced their opposition to it. I will explain these details further in this chapter.

Let's take a step back to 2008 when the UPA government was in power. On 6th May 2008, the government introduced the Women's Reservation Bill in the Lok Sabha. Just as Law Minister H. R. Bhardwaj was about to speak on the bill, something unprecedented happened. Samaj***i Party MP Abbu A*mi rushed forward, snatched a copy of the bill, and tore it apart. Another Sama***di Party MP then took the torn pieces and threw them across the Lok Sabha. This wasn't a scene from a movie, but a real event in the Indian Parliament.

Why did the Samaj***i Party react so strongly? To understand this, we need to delve into the reasons behind the introduction of this bill. The issue of reservation was a topic of discussion even before India gained independence. In 1931, Begum Shahnawaz and Sarojini Naidu wrote to the British Prime Minister to inquire about the status of women in India's new constitution. They argued that women did not need special treatment but rather their rightful place in society. When debates took place in the Constituent Assembly in 1946, the issue of women's reservation was once again brought to the forefront.

There were 15 women members in the Constituent Assembly, including prominent figures like Sarojini N***u, Renuka R**, Hansa M***a, and Vijayalakshmi Pa***t. However, during the debates, it became evident that not only did many male members oppose women's reservation, but several female members were also against it. They believed that women should be recognized based on merit, not through special treatment. Renuka R** articulated this sentiment by stating, "We don't want a reservation for women. We've always been against special treatment and reservations." She argued that reserving seats for women would undermine their abilities and that women, if given opportunities based on merit, would have a fair chance to succeed in a free India.

Other politicians, like H. V. Kamath, shared the view that women should participate in politics, but not through reservations. Some members had a different perspective, suggesting that government affairs require serious calculations and a calm mind, qualities they believed women lacked. Due to such debates, the idea of women's reservation was ultimately rejected by the Constituent Assembly.

However, this issue resurfaced in Indian politics years later. In 1974, the Committee on the Status of Women in India argued for increased representation of women in politics. While these reservations were not initially popular at the national level, several states began to take the initiative. This movement gained momentum nine years later, in 1983, Karnataka made a historic decision to become the first state in India to reserve 25% of seats for women in panchayati institutions.

Following this, the National Perspective Plan for Women recommended a 30% reservation for women. This was the first official government document to demand such a reservation. During this period, Rajiv Gandhi, who was the Prime Minister, placed a strong emphasis on panchayati institutions. He believed in decentralizing power through panchayats. The 73rd and 74th Amendments, introduced in 1993, were the first institutional steps to increase women's political participation in India. These amendments reserved one-third of the seats for women in Panchayati Raj institutions.

Today, 21 states in India have reserved 50% of seats for women in panchayati institutions, a significant outcome of these earlier reservations. We have gained significant insights into the impact of these reservations and the types of women who benefit from them. We will explore these details further later on. The story that began with panchayati institutions eventually made its way to the Parliament and state assemblies.

In 1996, Ramakant Kha**p, who was the Union Minister for Law and Justice at the time, received an important call from H.D. Devegowda, the newly appointed Prime Minister. The Prime Minister invited Khalap for a cup of coffee, during which he instructed him to prepare a Women's Reservation Bill. Deve Gowda was motivated to introduce this bill due to his long-standing commitment to increasing women's representation. As Chief Minister of Karnataka, he had implemented 33% reservation for women in government jobs and 50% reservation in educational institutions. Just three months into his tenure as Prime Minister, he directed his cabinet to discuss the Women's Reservation Bill.

On September 9, 1996, the bill was presented in the Lok Sabha, where only 40 out of 543 members were women. However, the government at the time was a coalition, known as the United Front, consisting of 13 political parties. The Prime Minister struggled to gain unanimous support from these parties to pass the bill. Consequently, the bill was referred to a Joint Select Committee, chaired by Geeta Mu**erjee of the Communist Party of India. Mukherjee later shared that she had received thousands of postcards, some written in blood, urging that the bill be passed during the Lok Sabha session.

The debate surrounding the bill often took unexpected turns. For instance, MP Sharad Yadav was a vocal opponent. He controversially commented on the type of women who would benefit from the reservation, suggesting that only urban and modern women with short hair would gain, while rural women would be left out. This kind of rhetoric highlighted the deep-seated concerns and biases that influenced the debate.

Ultimately, the bill failed to pass. Mary E. John, a professor at the Center for Women's Development Studies, pointed out that many politicians feared that reserving seats for women would inadvertently increase the representation of the general caste in Parliament. Two years later, the NDA government under Atal Bihari Vajpayee made another attempt to pass the bill. However, it once again faced strong opposition from leaders like Mulayam Singh Ya**v, Sharad Ya**v, and Lalu Pra**d Ya**v, who were staunchly against women's reservation.

The Vajpayee government made multiple attempts to pass the Women's Reservation Bill in 1999, 2002, and 2003. However, these efforts were met with significant challenges. In 1999, Jayalali**aa withdrew her support for the Vajpayee government, and later, parties like the Samaj**di Party insisted that they would only approve the bill if it included reservations for marginalized communities. Similar arguments resurfaced during UPA government, when Lalu Prasad Ya**v demanded quotas within the bill for OBC, ST, SC, and Muslim communities. Maya**ti, on the other hand, called for a separate reservation specifically for Dalit women.

Mulayam Singh Ya**v expressed a different concern, stating that if the Women's Reservation Bill were passed, it would lead to inappropriate behavior, such as young men in Parliament whistling at women. Yogi Aditya**th argued that reservations already existed in panchayats and questioned whether such reservations would impact child care. He suggested that the current experiment in panchayats should continue, and if proven successful, a quota could then be implemented in Parliament.

Despite these objections, BJP spokesperson Nirmala Sithara**n affirmed her party's support for the bill. Yet, the bill still failed to pass, even though both the Congress and BJP included it in their manifestos in 2014, pledging to pass it.

It wasn't until 2023 that the bill was finally passed, largely due to the BJP's significant political power in both the Lok Sabha and Rajya Sabha, which allowed them to overcome the hurdles that had previously blocked the bill.

The discussion surrounding the Women's Reservation Bill did not begin this year; it started back in 1996. It took over 25 years for the bill to finally gain approval. During this period, prominent leaders such as Lalu Pr***d Y*d*v and Yogi Adity***th voiced their opposition to it. I will explain these details further in this chapter.

Let's take a step back to 2008 when the UPA government was in power. On 6th May 2008, the government introduced the Women's Reservation Bill in the Lok Sabha. Just as Law Minister H. R. Bhardwaj was about to speak on the bill, something unprecedented happened. Samaj***i Party MP Abbu A*mi rushed forward, snatched a copy of the bill, and tore it apart. Another Sama***di Party MP then took the torn pieces and threw them across the Lok Sabha. This wasn't a scene from a movie, but a real event in the Indian Parliament.

Why did the Samaj***i Party react so strongly? To understand this, we need to delve into the reasons behind the introduction of this bill. The issue of reservation was a topic of discussion even before India gained independence. In 1931, Begum Shahnawaz and Sarojini Naidu wrote to the British Prime Minister to inquire about the status of women in India's new constitution. They argued that women did not need special treatment but rather their rightful place in society. When debates took place in the Constituent Assembly in 1946, the issue of women's reservation was once again brought to the forefront.

There were 15 women members in the Constituent Assembly, including prominent figures like Sarojini N***u, Renuka R**, Hansa M***a, and Vijayalakshmi Pa***t. However, during the debates, it became evident that not only did many male members oppose women's reservation, but several female members were also against it. They believed that women should be recognized based on merit, not through special treatment. Renuka R** articulated this sentiment by stating, "We don't want a reservation for women. We've always been against special treatment and reservations." She argued that reserving seats for women would undermine their abilities and that women, if given opportunities based on merit, would have a fair chance to succeed in a free India.

Other politicians, like H. V. Kamath, shared the view that women should participate in politics, but not through reservations. Some members had a different perspective, suggesting that government affairs require serious calculations and a calm mind, qualities they believed women lacked. Due to such debates, the idea of women's reservation was ultimately rejected by the Constituent Assembly.

However, this issue resurfaced in Indian politics years later. In 1974, the Committee on the Status of Women in India argued for increased representation of women in politics. While these reservations were not initially popular at the national level, several states began to take the initiative. This movement gained momentum nine years later, in 1983, Karnataka made a historic decision to become the first state in India to reserve 25% of seats for women in panchayati institutions.

Following this, the National Perspective Plan for Women recommended a 30% reservation for women. This was the first official government document to demand such a reservation. During this period, Rajiv Gandhi, who was the Prime Minister, placed a strong emphasis on panchayati institutions. He believed in decentralizing power through panchayats. The 73rd and 74th Amendments, introduced in 1993, were the first institutional steps to increase women's political participation in India. These amendments reserved one-third of the seats for women in Panchayati Raj institutions.

Today, 21 states in India have reserved 50% of seats for women in panchayati institutions, a significant outcome of these earlier reservations. We have gained significant insights into the impact of these reservations and the types of women who benefit from them. We will explore these details further later on. The story that began with panchayati institutions eventually made its way to the Parliament and state assemblies.

In 1996, Ramakant Kha**p, who was the Union Minister for Law and Justice at the time, received an important call from H.D. Devegowda, the newly appointed Prime Minister. The Prime Minister invited Khalap for a cup of coffee, during which he instructed him to prepare a Women's Reservation Bill. Deve Gowda was motivated to introduce this bill due to his long-standing commitment to increasing women's representation. As Chief

Minister of Karnataka, he had implemented 33% reservation for women in government jobs and 50% reservation in educational institutions. Just three months into his tenure as Prime Minister, he directed his cabinet to discuss the Women's Reservation Bill.

On September 9, 1996, the bill was presented in the Lok Sabha, where only 40 out of 543 members were women. However, the government at the time was a coalition, known as the United Front, consisting of 13 political parties. The Prime Minister struggled to gain unanimous support from these parties to pass the bill. Consequently, the bill was referred to a Joint Select Committee, chaired by Geeta Mu**erjee of the Communist Party of India. Mukherjee later shared that she had received thousands of postcards, some written in blood, urging that the bill be passed during the Lok Sabha session.

The debate surrounding the bill often took unexpected turns. For instance, MP Sharad Yadav was a vocal opponent. He controversially commented on the type of women who would benefit from the reservation, suggesting that only urban and modern women with short hair would gain, while rural women would be left out. This kind of rhetoric highlighted the deep-seated concerns and biases that influenced the debate.

Ultimately, the bill failed to pass. Mary E. John, a professor at the Center for Women's Development Studies, pointed out that many politicians feared that reserving seats for women would inadvertently increase the representation of the general caste in Parliament. Two years later, the NDA government under Atal Bihari Vajpayee made another attempt to pass the bill. However, it once again faced strong opposition from leaders like Mulayam Singh Ya**v, Sharad Ya**v, and Lalu Pra**d Ya**v, who were staunchly against women's reservation.

The Vajpayee government made multiple attempts to pass the Women's Reservation Bill in 1999, 2002, and 2003. However, these efforts were met with significant challenges. In 1999, Jayalali**aa withdrew her support for the Vajpayee government, and later, parties like the Samaj**di Party insisted that they would only approve the bill if it included reservations for marginalized communities. Similar arguments resurfaced during UPA government, when Lalu Prasad Ya**v demanded quotas within the bill for OBC, ST, SC, and Muslim communities. Maya**ti, on the other hand, called for a separate reservation specifically for Dalit women.

Mulayam Singh Ya**v expressed a different concern, stating that if the Women's Reservation Bill were passed, it would lead to inappropriate behavior, such as young men in Parliament whistling at women. Yogi

Aditya**th argued that reservations already existed in panchayats and questioned whether such reservations would impact child care. He suggested that the current experiment in panchayats should continue, and if proven successful, a quota could then be implemented in Parliament.

Despite these objections, BJP spokesperson Nirmala Sithara**n affirmed her party's support for the bill. Yet, the bill still failed to pass, even though both the Congress and BJP included it in their manifestos in 2014, pledging to pass it.

It wasn't until 2023 that the bill was finally passed, largely due to the BJP's significant political power in both the Lok Sabha and Rajya Sabha, which allowed them to overcome the hurdles that had previously blocked the bill.

What is the bill exactly?

The bill, now a historic piece of legislation, mandates that 33% of seats in the Lok Sabha and state legislative assemblies will be reserved for women, marking a significant step toward increasing women's representation in Indian politics.

The Women's Reservation Bill also includes seats reserved specifically for Scheduled Caste (SC) and Scheduled Tribe (ST) women. This means that within the overall reservation for women, there is an additional layer of quotas for SC and ST women, often referred to as a "quota within a quota." The bill states that these reservations will be valid for 15 years, after which Parliament can decide whether to extend them.

The Union Law Minister has highlighted that this bill will increase the number of women in Parliament from 82 to 181. However, the implementation of this bill will not happen immediately. Two key prerequisites are needed: the census and delimitation.

In India, a census is conducted every 10 years, with the last one occurring in 2011. The next census was scheduled for 2021, but due to the COVID-19 pandemic, it was delayed. According to government sources, the next census is expected to take place in late 2024. Once completed, the census will provide updated population data for each state, which is crucial for the process of delimitation.

Delimitation refers to the allocation of Lok Sabha seats to each state based on its population. As the population changes, so too must the political map, as the Indian Constitution mandates that the population of each constituency should be nearly equal. This means that when the population data is updated, the number and distribution of seats in the Lok Sabha will also change.

It is estimated that the total number of seats in the Lok Sabha could increase from 543 to 753. This would likely result in more seats being allocated to states with larger populations, such as Uttar Pradesh and Bihar, thereby increasing the political influence of North Indian states and reducing that of South Indian states. This potential shift in power is a significant concern for Southern states.

Given these steps—first the census, then delimitation—it is anticipated that the Women's Reservation Bill will not be implemented until around 2029. The census starting in late 2024 may take up to two years to complete, meaning that delimitation could occur in 2029. Thus, the reservations will begin in 2029, not immediately.

Now, the main issue to consider is whether these reservations will benefit the country and its women. We must also recognize the political impact of this bill, as it will present significant challenges for political parties in adapting to these changes.

If the Lok Sabha expands to 750 seats in the next six years, political parties will need to find 250 women to become Members of Parliament. This presents a challenge: how can parties develop a strong bench of qualified women candidates? One effective approach is to look to the panchayats, the grassroots level of India's political system.

In 2010, Yogi Aditya***h suggested that before implementing reservations in Parliament, we should first assess how they work in panchayats. Fortunately, there has been extensive research on this topic, allowing us to evaluate the impact of women's reservations in these local bodies.

The introduction of reservations in panchayats had three main objectives. We can measure the success of these reservations by assessing their impact on each objective:

1. Increase in Women's Representation: The goal was to ensure that more women, not just proxy candidates, were elected to leadership positions.

2. Addressing Women's Issues: The aim was for these women leaders to raise and address issues that directly affect women, thus ensuring that the government prioritizes women's concerns.

3. Changing Societal Perceptions: The ultimate goal was to change society's perception of women by proving their capability and reducing the long-term need for reservations.

Now, let's examine the first objective—whether women's representation in panchayats has truly increased or if it has been overshadowed by proxy candidates. An example from three years ago in the Attari Gram Panchayat highlights this issue. On every wall, you would see "Anil Yad*v, the Gram Pradhan of 2019" written. However, Anil Yad*v was not the actual Gram Pradhan; his mother held that position. When questioned, Anil explained that he was simply representing his mother, executing her orders. He claimed that his mother made all the decisions.

This scenario is not unique. When villagers were asked about women in leadership roles, many said that in cases where a woman holds a position of power, 75% of the work is actually done by her husband, son, or father-in-law. In India, there's even a term for this phenomenon: "Pati Pradhan," which refers to a husband who effectively acts as the leader while his wife holds the official title.

This example underscores the challenges of truly increasing women's representation and ensuring that they are not merely figureheads, but actual leaders who drive change. A minister in Punjab discovered that many women Sarpanchs (village heads) don't even attend their meetings. This observation is backed by research, which found that 17% of the husbands of women Pradhans were former Pradhans or councillors themselves, suggesting a continuation of power within families. Additionally, 43% of these women reported that their husbands regularly assisted them in their official duties, raising concerns about the authenticity of their leadership.

Moreover, 89% of women Pradhans had not participated in any Panchayat activities before assuming their roles, indicating a lack of prior political experience or engagement. When compared to their male counterparts, these women often had lower levels of education and less political experience. This has led to fears that similar patterns could emerge in Parliament if the Women's Reservation Bill is implemented, with women possibly becoming figureheads rather than true decision-makers.

According to Varad Tikam

I understand your concerns about the potential misuse of the Women's Reservation Bill, similar to what has been observed in Gram Panchayat elections. The risk of women becoming figureheads rather than genuine leaders is a legitimate issue. As I mentioned, this could undermine the intended purpose of the bill and instead serve as a tool for creating a vote bank rather than fostering true merit-based leadership.

Your preference for a merit-based system is valid, as many believe that positions of power should be earned through experience, capability, and dedication rather than through reservations. The challenge lies in finding a balance between providing opportunities for underrepresented groups and ensuring that those opportunities lead to genuine leadership and positive change.

The effectiveness of this bill will largely depend on its implementation and the safeguards put in place to ensure that it truly empowers women rather than simply reinforcing existing power structures.

CHAPTER THIRTEEN

NEED OF COMPLETE BAN ON TOBACCO

Introduction

Tobacco has become a silent killer, claiming the lives of 1.35 million people globally each year. In India, the situation is equally dire, with 3,699 deaths occurring daily, and 154 people losing their lives every hour due to tobacco-related causes. These staggering numbers reveal the devastating impact of tobacco on public health. Despite widespread awareness of the dangers of tobacco, 30% of India's population, amounting to 194 million people, continues to consume it. The alarming statistics underscore the urgent need to address this public health crisis comprehensively.

The Persistence of Smokeless Tobacco

India's battle with tobacco is compounded by the widespread use of smokeless tobacco. Despite a ban on smokeless tobacco in India, 21.4% of adults continue to use it, resulting in over 200,000 deaths annually. This raises a critical question: how does a banned substance continue to be so widely available? The answer lies in the deep-rooted and systematic exploitation of legal loopholes and the involvement of powerful stakeholders, from celebrities to politicians, who prioritize profit over public health.

The Influence of Advertising and Celebrities

Tobacco consumption is not an innate behavior; it is learned and influenced by the environment, including the media and advertising. In the past, tobacco advertisements were pervasive on television, featuring prominent celebrities who glamorized smoking and tobacco use. Although direct advertising of tobacco products has been banned in India since the introduction of the Cable Television Network Regulation Act in 1995, tobacco companies have found other ways to promote their products. They have turned to surrogate advertising, where they market seemingly harmless products like pan masala and elaichi, which are associated with tobacco products, to continue influencing consumers subtly.

Government Regulations and Loopholes

In response to the growing tobacco epidemic, the Indian government has implemented several measures. The Cigarettes and Other Tobacco Products Act (COTPA) was introduced to regulate tobacco consumption, banning smoking in public places, prohibiting the sale of tobacco products within 100 yards of educational institutions, and restricting tobacco use by individuals under 18 years of age. Despite these efforts, tobacco companies have found ways to circumvent the regulations, such as selling pan masala and tobacco in separate packets, allowing consumers to mix them and recreate the banned product, Gutkha.

The Role of Celebrities in Promoting Tobacco

The involvement of celebrities in promoting tobacco products is particularly concerning. Big names in Bollywood, have endorsed pan masala brands that are closely associated with tobacco. These endorsements not only undermine public health efforts but also send a dangerous message to young, impressionable audiences. The influence of celebrities is powerful, and their involvement in such campaigns contributes significantly to the ongoing tobacco crisis.

Economic Implications of Tobacco Consumption

The tobacco industry is often defended on economic grounds, with proponents arguing that it generates significant revenue for the government. In 2020, the Indian government generated Rs 53,750 crore in tax revenue from tobacco products. However, this argument overlooks the far greater economic costs associated with tobacco-related illnesses. In 2017, the Indian government spent Rs 2 lakh crore on healthcare expenses related to tobacco diseases, amounting to 1.4% of the nation's GDP. For every Rs 100 earned from tobacco taxes, Rs 816 is spent on healthcare costs, making tobacco a net loss to the economy

The Human Cost of Tobacco

The most tragic aspect of the tobacco crisis is its impact on the poor and vulnerable populations. The majority of tobacco users in India are from low-income backgrounds, where tobacco use is often driven by economic necessity. Many laborers consume tobacco to suppress hunger, allowing them to work longer hours. This creates a vicious cycle of poverty, addiction, and disease, where the most vulnerable members of society bear the brunt of the health and economic consequences.

According to Author Varad Tikam

I firmly believe that India must take a bold and decisive step by implementing a complete ban on the distribution and consumption of tobacco within our nation. While the production of tobacco could continue, it should be strictly for export purposes, with no exception allowing its sale or consumption within India. This is not just a matter of public health but a moral responsibility to protect future generations from the devastating effects of tobacco.

To enforce this ban, possession of tobacco should be considered a grave offense, warranting the harshest penalties, including life imprisonment. Such stringent measures are essential to send a clear message that the well-being of our citizens is paramount and that we will not tolerate any violations of this law.

The transportation of tobacco from the factory to the warehouse, and subsequently from the warehouse to the port, should be tightly controlled. Only those with a special government-issued license should be permitted to handle such activities, ensuring that every movement of tobacco within the country is accounted for and monitored. Each shipment must be accompanied by a detailed invoice, specifying the quantity, destination, and purpose, with regular audits to ensure compliance.

Security at warehouses where tobacco is stored must be fortified with 24/7 surveillance, employing both advanced technology and on-ground personnel. This is critical to prevent any unauthorized access or diversion of tobacco products into the domestic market. The warehouses should be treated as high-security zones, with multiple layers of security checks and stringent protocols for anyone entering or exiting the premises.

Execution of this plan will require a dedicated task force with the authority to conduct inspections, enforce the law, and take swift action against violators. This task force should be empowered to work in coordination with customs officials, local law enforcement, and even international agencies to ensure that the entire supply chain is transparent and secure.

In addition, a robust public awareness campaign should be launched to educate citizens about the new law, the dangers of tobacco, and the severe consequences of illegal possession or consumption. This will not only reinforce the importance of the ban but also encourage public cooperation in reporting any violations

By implementing these measures, we can take a significant step toward safeguarding the health of our nation and setting an example for the world in our commitment to eradicating the scourge of tobacco. This is not just about enforcement; it's about building a healthier, stronger India for the generations to come.

CHAPTER FOURTEEN

HOW SHOULD INDIA GET PAKISTAN-OCCUPIED KASHMIR BACK

The Kashmir issue has always been a pivotal aspect of India-Pakistan relations. The abrogation of Article 370 on August 5, 2019, by a Presidential Order marked a significant turning point in the status of Jammu and Kashmir. This article previously granted special autonomy to the region, yet a considerable portion of the territory remains under Pakistan's control since its violent annexation in 1947. This region, known in India as Pakistan-Occupied Kashmir (PoK), comprises approximately 30% of Jammu and Kashmir, covering 2.22 lakh square kilometers, with a small section (5,180 square kilometers) having been ceded to China.

The Division of Kashmir

Pakistan-Occupied Kashmir is divided by Pakistan into two administrative regions: Azad Jammu and Kashmir (AJK), and Gilgit-Baltistan. The capital of AJK is Muzaffarabad, situated on the Neelam River (known as Kishanganga in India). Gilgit-Baltistan, covering about 65,000 square kilometers, is a strategically significant area under Pakistan's control. The region is known for its rugged terrain, hosting over 250 mountain peaks, including some of the world's longest glaciers outside the polar regions.

The Accession of Jammu and Kashmir to India

In 1947, during the partition of India, the princely states were given the option to join either India or Pakistan or remain independent. Maharaja Hari Singh, the ruler of Jammu and Kashmir, faced immense pressure from both India and Pakistan, as well as internal strife within his kingdom. In response to an uprising fueled by oppressive taxation, tribal militias from Pakistan's North-West Frontier Province, with the support of the Pakistani military, invaded Jammu and Kashmir. As they advanced towards Srinagar, Maharaja Hari Singh sought military assistance from India.

On October 26, 1947, Maharaja Hari Singh signed the Instrument of Accession, formally acceding Jammu and Kashmir to India. This agreement transferred control of defense, foreign affairs, and communications to India. The Indian Army swiftly intervened, pushing back the invading forces, but a significant portion of the region had already fallen into Pakistani hands, resulting in the division of Kashmir.

The Role of the United Nations

The Jammu and Kashmir issue was brought before the United Nations by Indian Prime Minister Jawaharlal Nehru on January 1, 1948. The UN passed Resolution 47, calling for the withdrawal of Pakistani forces from Jammu and Kashmir and urging India to maintain a minimal military presence in the region. However, Pakistan's refusal to comply with the resolution led to the failure of the proposed plebiscite. The ceasefire line established by the Karachi Agreement in 1949 became the Line of Control (LoC), which still serves as the de facto border between the two countries.

Strategic Importance of PoK

Pakistan-Occupied Kashmir holds immense strategic value due to its geographic location. It shares borders with several countries, including Pakistan, Afghanistan (via the Wakhan Corridor), and China. The region is also rich in natural resources, particularly fresh water and hydroelectric potential. The China-Pakistan Economic Corridor (CPEC), a multi-billion-dollar project, passes through Gilgit-Baltistan, further enhancing its geopolitical significance. This development poses a significant threat to India's security and its strategic interests in the region.

The Challenges of Reclaiming PoK

India has faced numerous challenges in its efforts to reclaim Pakistan-occupied Kashmir. The region's mountainous terrain makes military operations difficult, while Pakistan's control over the area allows for easy access and defense. India's policy of "no first use" of nuclear weapons has also restrained its ability to launch offensive operations. Moreover, the presence of a pro-Pakistan sentiment among a section of the local population complicates efforts to integrate the region fully into India. I have written about this issue of "no first use" policy in a different chapter in an elaborated form

International Dynamics and the Role of China

China's involvement in the region further complicates the situation. In 1963, Pakistan ceded a part of Gilgit-Baltistan to China, strengthening their strategic partnership. The CPEC project has cemented China's influence in the region, making it a crucial player in the Kashmir issue. Any attempt by India to reclaim PoK would likely face resistance from both Pakistan and China, two nuclear-armed states.

Solutions according to Varad Tikam

The issue of Pakistan-Occupied Kashmir (PoK) has been a persistent thorn in the side of India's national security and territorial integrity since the partition of 1947. Over the decades, PoK has not only been a flashpoint for military conflicts between India and Pakistan but also a significant factor in the geopolitical dynamics of South Asia. As India continues to assert its claim over the entire region of Jammu and Kashmir, it faces the challenge of strategically addressing the situation in PoK. This chapter delves into the various strategic options available to India for reclaiming PoK, emphasizing the importance of a multifaceted approach that includes diplomatic, political, and military strategies.

Establishing a PoK Administration in Exile

One of the most significant steps India could take is the establishment of a PoK administration in exile. This move would not only underscore India's claim over the region but also provide a voice to those displaced by Pakistan's illegal occupation.

International Recognition and Legitimacy

The creation of an official PoK administration in exile would draw global attention to the region's plight. Such a government-in-exile would serve as a legitimate body that challenges Pakistan's authority in PoK, thereby strengthening India's narrative on the international stage. This administration could highlight human rights violations, economic exploitation, and the lack of political freedom under Pakistani control, thereby garnering sympathy and support from the international community.

Support from PoK Refugees

A PoK administration in exile could also galvanize support from the refugee community, providing them with a platform to express their grievances and aspirations. This would not only consolidate India's position but also serve as a testament to its commitment to the people of PoK. By aligning with these refugees, India could also build a more robust narrative against Pakistan's occupation, further solidifying its claim over the region.

Reserved Legislative Assembly Seats for PoK

Another strategic option is the activation of the reserved seats in the Jammu and Kashmir Legislative Assembly for representatives from PoK. Under the Jammu and Kashmir Representation of the People Act, several seats are reserved for PoK, which remain vacant due to the region being under Pakistani control.

Democratic Representation

Filling these seats would be a powerful political statement, demonstrating India's commitment to the democratic process and its inclusive approach to governance. This move would engage the PoK population in India's political system, providing them with a formal channel to participate in the governance of the region, even from afar.

Political Engagement and International Advocacy

By involving representatives from PoK in the legislative process, India would be able to articulate the aspirations and concerns of the PoK population more effectively on international platforms. These representatives could serve as powerful advocates in international forums, lobbying for support and drawing attention to the injustices faced by the people of PoK under Pakistani occupation.

Engaging with the Population of Gilgit-Baltistan

Gilgit-Baltistan, a region of PoK, has historically been marginalized by Pakistan and subjected to discriminatory policies. India could focus on engaging with the population of Gilgit-Baltistan to build support for its stance on the region.

Supporting Pro-India Activism

India can amplify the voices of pro-India activists in Gilgit-Baltistan, who often face persecution by Pakistani authorities. Offering asylum or a platform to these activists could help India build a network of supporters within PoK, advocating for reunification with India. By doing so, India could create a counter-narrative to Pakistan's control over the region.

Strengthening Cultural and Economic Ties

India could also work to strengthen cultural and economic ties with the people of Gilgit-Baltistan. By emphasizing historical connections and offering economic incentives, such as scholarships or trade opportunities, India could foster goodwill and create a more favorable environment for its strategic goals in the region.

Raising International Awareness

India can bring international attention to the human rights abuses and lack of autonomy in Gilgit-Baltistan through diplomatic channels and global media. Highlighting these issues could garner international support and apply pressure on Pakistan to address the grievances of the region's people.

Diplomatic and Strategic Alliances

India's diplomatic relationships with global powers and regional allies play a crucial role in its strategy for PoK. Building strong alliances can help India garner international support and counterbalance Pakistan's influence.

Engagement with the United States

India's growing strategic partnership with the United States could be a significant asset in addressing the PoK issue. By aligning with U.S. interests in the region, particularly concerning Afghanistan and counter-terrorism, India could secure U.S. support in international forums, including the United Nations. This support would be crucial in countering Pakistan's narrative and applying diplomatic pressure on Islamabad.

Collaboration with Quad Nations

India's involvement in the Quad (Quadrilateral Security Dialogue) with the U.S., Japan, and Australia provides another avenue for garnering international support. The Quad's focus on a free and open Indo-Pacific region aligns with India's strategic interests and could extend to the issue of PoK. This collaboration would enhance India's ability to influence global opinion on PoK.

Balancing China's Influence

China's involvement in Gilgit-Baltistan through the China-Pakistan Economic Corridor (CPEC) presents a significant challenge to India's strategic goals in PoK. India must engage diplomatically with China to address concerns related to CPEC and its implications for Jammu and Kashmir's sovereignty. Reopening diplomatic dialogues with China could help mitigate the risks associated with Chinese investments in the region.

Leveraging International Law

India can also strengthen its case for PoK by taking legal action in international forums, emphasizing Pakistan's violation of the Shimla Agreement and UN resolutions. Building a strong legal case, supported by historical documents and international law, could further legitimize India's claim to PoK on the global stage.

Military Preparedness and Strategic Calculations

While India has traditionally adhered to a policy of "no first use" concerning nuclear weapons and avoided offensive military operations in PoK, changing dynamics in the region may require a review of military strategies.

Enhanced Military Presence

India could bolster its military presence along the Line of Control (LoC) to deter Pakistani aggression and be prepared for potential opportunities to reclaim PoK. This would involve enhancing infrastructure, deploying advanced surveillance systems, and maintaining a high state of readiness to respond to any developments in the region.

Use of Special Forces

India could consider utilizing its special forces to conduct targeted operations against terror camps in PoK, similar to past surgical strikes. These actions would serve as a deterrent to Pakistan and demonstrate India's capability to protect its interests in the region.

Psychological Warfare and Information Operations

India could engage in psychological operations and information warfare to undermine Pakistan's control over PoK. This could involve broadcasting pro-India content, supporting anti-Pakistan movements within PoK, and using cyber capabilities to disrupt Pakistan's operations in the region.

Engaging with the United Nations

India should continue to advocate for reforms within the United Nations Security Council and other bodies to reflect the changing global power dynamics. By pushing for a more prominent role in these institutions, India could secure a stronger platform to address the PoK issue and garner international support for its position.

Human Rights Advocacy

India can work closely with international human rights organizations to document and expose the human rights violations occurring in PoK. By providing detailed accounts of Pakistan's actions in the region, India could strengthen its case in the international community and apply pressure on Pakistan to address these issues.

Economic Sanctions and Trade Leverage

India could lobby for economic sanctions against Pakistan for its illegal occupation and human rights abuses in PoK. Additionally, India could use its economic relationships with other countries to apply diplomatic pressure on Pakistan, leveraging trade deals and investments to gain support for its stance on PoK.

Conclusion

Reclaiming Pakistan-Occupied Kashmir (PoK) is a complex challenge that requires a comprehensive and multifaceted approach. India must carefully balance diplomatic, political, and military strategies while engaging with international allies and building support among the local population in PoK. While the task is daunting, with careful planning and international cooperation, India can strengthen its position and work towards integrating PoK into the Indian Union. The strategic options outlined in this chapter provide a roadmap for India to navigate the geopolitical complexities surrounding PoK and work towards a resolution that aligns with its national interests.

CHAPTER FIFTEEN

THE REALITY OF MOHANDAS KARAMCHAND GANDHI

Introduction

Mahatma Gandhi is often revered as the father of the Indian nation, a symbol of peace, and a proponent of non-violence. His legacy, however, is complex and layered with aspects that many of his devotees and admirers may find unsettling. Jawaharlal Nehru, a close associate and admirer of Gandhi, once remarked to filmmaker Richard Attenborough that while Gandhi was a great man, he was not without his weaknesses. Gandhi himself emphasized the importance of criticism, acknowledging that no one, not even a revered leader, should be beyond reproach. In this chapter, we delve into four lesser-known aspects of Gandhi's life: his experiments with sex, his dealings with racism, his views on the caste system, and his economic policies.

Is Gandhi the "Father of the Nation"?

While Mahatma Gandhi is widely honored as the "Father of the Nation" in India, this title lacks official recognition. A Right to Information (RTI) query revealed that there is no formal document or governmental order designating Gandhi as such. This response underscores that, despite Gandhi's immense contributions to India's independence and his revered status, the title "Father of the Nation" is more a matter of popular sentiment than official acknowledgment. In light of this, there is a growing argument that there should be a ban on the use of such titles and the dissemination of misinformation. This would ensure that public discourse is based on verified information and reflects a more accurate portrayal of historical figures, rather than perpetuating unverified or exaggerated claims.

Gandhi's Experiments with Sex

Gandhi's views on sex and his experiments in this domain are perhaps among the most controversial aspects of his life. Gandhi took a vow of celibacy in 1906, determined to master his desires and focus on his spiritual and political work. However, this vow led to peculiar and ethically questionable experiments later in his life.

In 1946, Gandhi began an experiment where he slept naked with young girls, including his grandnieces, Manu and Abha. These young women, who were about 60 years younger than Gandhi, were often referred to as Gandhi's "walking sticks" due to the support they provided him in his later years. The purpose of these experiments, according to Gandhi, was to test his self-control and demonstrate his ability to resist sexual arousal, even in the presence of naked women.

These experiments shocked many of Gandhi's close associates. His stenographer and Bengali translator, both disturbed by the knowledge of Gandhi's behavior, left him in protest. The Indian media, however, largely remained silent on the matter, avoiding public discussion of Gandhi's private life.

Gandhi's rationale for these experiments was rooted in his belief that mastering one's sexual desires was crucial to achieving spiritual purity. He believed that if a man could lie with naked women without feeling aroused, it would prove his complete self-control. Gandhi's personal history, particularly an incident from his youth, may have influenced these views. At 16, while his father was dying, Gandhi left his father's side to have sex with his wife, Kasturba. This event haunted him throughout his life, leading him to view sexual desire as something that could cloud judgment and lead to regret.

Gandhi also held strong opinions against contraceptives, arguing that their use indicated a lack of self-discipline. He feared that widespread use of contraceptives would lead to a society obsessed with sex, ultimately resulting in moral decay. While Gandhi's views on sex were shared by some during his time, his methods and experiments remain controversial and difficult to justify.

Gandhi's Interaction with Racism

Gandhi's time in South Africa is often highlighted as a period that shaped his philosophy of non-violence and civil disobedience. However, his interactions with racism during this time reveal a more complex and troubling side of his beliefs.

In 1893, at the age of 24, Gandhi traveled to South Africa to work as a legal representative for an Indian trader. He spent 21 years there, during which he experienced racial discrimination firsthand. The infamous incident where Gandhi was thrown off a train for sitting in a "whites-only" compartment is often cited as a pivotal moment that inspired his activism. However, Gandhi's response to racism was not as straightforward as many would believe.

While Gandhi was outraged at being discriminated against as an Indian, he was also deeply offended by being associated with black Africans, whom he referred to as "kaffirs" and "infidels" in his writings. Gandhi believed that Indians, being of Indo-Aryan descent, were superior to black Africans and should be treated as equals to the British, rather than being lumped together with Africans.

In letters to the South African colonial authorities, Gandhi argued for the recognition of Indians as part of the "civilized" races, distinct from the black population. He used derogatory language to describe black Africans, calling them "dirty" and "uncivilized." Even as he aged, Gandhi continued to hold these views, though some scholars argue that his opinions evolved over time. However, many African scholars dispute this, pointing to evidence that Gandhi's racist attitudes persisted well into his later years.

Gandhi's legacy in Africa remains contentious, with his statue being removed from the University of Ghana in recent years. For many, his early racist views undermine his status as a universal icon of equality and justice.

Gandhi's Views on the Caste System

Gandhi's approach to the caste system in India is another area where his beliefs have sparked significant debate. While Gandhi is often credited with advocating for the rights of Dalits and fighting against untouchability, his views on the caste system as a whole were more nuanced and, at times, contradictory.

Dr. B.R. Ambedkar, the principal architect of the Indian Constitution and a staunch opponent of the caste system, criticized Gandhi for what he perceived as a double standard. Ambedkar argued that Gandhi did not genuinely want to abolish the caste system but rather sought to reform it in a way that maintained its structure. Gandhi believed that the caste system had a role in preserving the order and strength of Hindu society. He opposed untouchability but did not advocate for the complete eradication of the caste hierarchy.

Gandhi's article, "The Ideal Bhangi," provides insight into his thoughts on the caste system. In it, he praised the role of bhangis (sanitation workers) in society, emphasizing the importance of their work in maintaining public health. However, his idealization of this role suggested an acceptance of the caste-based division of labor, rather than a rejection of the system that enforced such roles.

Gandhi also opposed inter-caste marriages, further highlighting his belief in the preservation of caste boundaries. This stance put him at odds with Ambedkar, who sought to dismantle the caste system altogether. The disagreement between Gandhi and Ambedkar came to a head during the negotiations over separate electorates for Dalits. Gandhi opposed the idea, fearing it would further divide Indian society, leading to the Poona Pact of 1932, which reserved seats for Dalits but within the general electorate.

In modern India, the caste system has evolved and, in many ways, lost its original meaning. The Varna system, from which the caste system was derived, was originally based on occupation rather than birth. Gandhi's failure to fully reject the caste system, despite his efforts to uplift the Dalits, remains a point of contention in discussions about his legacy.

According to Varad Tikam

In my view, it is crucial to address the misconceptions surrounding Mahatma Gandhi's legacy with clarity and honesty. While Gandhi played a significant role in India's freedom struggle, he was not the sole architect of our independence. His philosophy of non-violence, though noble, may have inadvertently delayed our freedom by placing constraints on more immediate and forceful forms of resistance. I firmly believe that the teachings of the Bhagavad Gita, where Krishna advises Arjuna to "perform your duty and fight" against injustice, highlight that sometimes, resistance requires more than mere non-violence. This perspective suggests that Gandhi's approach, while influential, was not the only or necessarily the most effective path to liberation.

Furthermore, I advocate for a ban on misinformation and the unfounded titles of "Father of the Nation" and "Mahatma" being conferred upon Gandhi. Such titles are not officially sanctioned and their continued use contributes to a distorted view of history. Additionally, I argue that October 2nd, Gandhi's birthday, should not be a public holiday. This day should instead be an opportunity for reflection on all facets of our history, recognizing both Gandhi's contributions and the broader spectrum of efforts and ideologies that shaped our nation. By reassessing and contextualizing Gandhi's role, I honour his legacy while also acknowledging the complex realities of our struggle for freedom.

ILLEGAL IMMIGRATION IN INDIA

Illegal immigration has been a persistent and growing concern for India, affecting its national security, economic stability, and social fabric. While much of the focus has been on the influx of immigrants from Bangladesh, the issue is compounded by the challenges posed by Pakistan, particularly in the context of cross-border terrorism and infiltration. This chapter delves into the historical and contemporary dimensions of illegal immigration from both Bangladesh and Pakistan, exploring the socio-political impacts, the response from the Indian government, and the need for a robust, multi-layered strategy to address this pressing issue.

The Bangladeshi Influx: A Historical Perspective

Since the formation of Bangladesh in 1971, illegal immigration into India has been a continuous issue. The roots of this problem can be traced back to the Bangladesh Liberation War, when millions of refugees fled to India. Over time, what began as a humanitarian crisis evolved into a significant demographic shift, particularly in the border states of West Bengal and the Northeast.

The porous 4,096-kilometer-long India-Bangladesh border is considered one of the most complex international boundaries in the world, making it an ideal route for illegal immigrants. Despite ongoing efforts since 1986 to fence the border, challenges such as difficult terrain, riverine boundaries, and political pressures have hindered complete border security. Consequently, illegal immigrants from Bangladesh have continued to cross into India, with estimates suggesting that millions reside illegally across the country.

The impact of this influx has been profound. In states like Assam and Tripura, the demographic balance has shifted, leading to tensions between indigenous communities and the growing immigrant population. The pressure on land, resources, and employment has sparked social unrest, contributing to the rise of insurgent groups and communal violence. The economic burden on the northeastern states is significant, as government resources intended for local development are diverted to manage the increasing population.

The Pakistani Element: A Strategic Threat

While Bangladesh's illegal immigration is primarily driven by economic factors, the challenge posed by Pakistan is more insidious, involving elements of cross-border terrorism, infiltration, and political destabilization. Pakistan has long used illegal immigration and infiltration as tools of its asymmetric warfare strategy against India.

The 3,323-kilometer-long India-Pakistan border, which includes the volatile Line of Control (LoC) in Jammu and Kashmir, is a hotspot for infiltration by militants trained and supported by the Pakistani military and intelligence agencies. These infiltrators often enter India disguised as refugees or economic migrants, blending in with local populations. The porous borders in states like Punjab and Rajasthan are also exploited for smuggling arms, drugs, and counterfeit currency, further destabilizing the region.

The involvement of Pakistan in fomenting unrest in India is well-documented. The infiltration of militants across the border has led to numerous terrorist attacks, causing significant loss of life and property. The situation in Kashmir, in particular, has been exacerbated by Pakistan's support for separatist movements, which are bolstered by the influx of illegal immigrants and infiltrators.

The Socio-Political Impact

The combined effect of illegal immigration from Bangladesh and Pakistan has been profound, particularly in the border regions. In the Northeast, the influx of Bangladeshi immigrants has altered the demographic landscape, leading to social tensions and conflicts over resources. Indigenous communities feel increasingly marginalized as their political and cultural dominance erodes. The rise of militant groups like the United Liberation Front of Asom (ULFA) can be partly attributed to these demographic changes, as local populations resist the perceived threat to their identity.

In the western and northern regions, the infiltration of militants from Pakistan has fueled terrorism and insurgency. The presence of illegal immigrants from Pakistan in states like Jammu and Kashmir has complicated the security situation, as they often provide logistical support to terrorist networks. The use of fake documents, including Indian voting cards, by these infiltrators further complicates efforts to identify and deport them.

The political ramifications of illegal immigration are significant. In many cases, illegal immigrants have been used as a vote bank by local politicians, who grant them voter IDs and other identity documents in exchange for electoral support. This practice undermines the integrity of the electoral process and exacerbates social divisions.

Author's views

Successive Indian governments have grappled with the issue of illegal immigration, but the response has often been inadequate. While measures like the National Register of Citizens (NRC) in Assam have been implemented to identify and deport illegal immigrants, the process has been fraught with challenges. The lack of clear data, political opposition, and logistical hurdles have made it difficult to achieve meaningful results.

In the case of Pakistan, the Indian government has focused on strengthening border security and countering infiltration. The deployment of advanced surveillance technology, construction of fences along the LoC, and the use of the Border Security Force (BSF) have helped to some extent, but the porous nature of the border and the ongoing hostility from Pakistan continue to pose significant challenges.

A comprehensive approach is needed to address the issue of illegal immigration from both Bangladesh and Pakistan. This approach should include not only enhanced border security but also diplomatic efforts to engage with the governments of these countries. For Bangladesh, this means working together to curb illegal migration and addressing the root causes of economic displacement. For Pakistan, it requires a firm stance against cross-border terrorism and infiltration, backed by international pressure.

As I reflect on the challenges of illegal immigration in India, I recognize the profound impact it has on our nation's security, economy, and social fabric. India's vast and diverse borders, coupled with evolving migration patterns and socio-economic pressures, present a complex problem that demands a comprehensive response.

I believe that addressing illegal immigration requires a multi-faceted strategy, one that encompasses not only enhanced border control but also tighter visa regulations, robust enforcement strategies, and international cooperation. It is essential for us to confront the root causes of migration, including economic instability and humanitarian crises, to develop a balanced and effective approach.

In this chapter, I will delve into each of these critical areas, providing a detailed framework for managing and mitigating the effects of illegal immigration. By modernizing our border infrastructure, streamlining visa processes, and strengthening our enforcement measures, we can create a more secure and stable immigration system. Engaging in international collaboration and addressing the underlying factors driving migration will further support these efforts.

Through this comprehensive strategy, I am confident that we can not only tackle the immediate challenges of illegal immigration but also lay the groundwork for long-term solutions. My goal is to offer a clear and actionable plan that will contribute to a more secure and prosperous future for India.

Solutions according to Varad Tikam

1. Enhancing Border Control

The effectiveness of border control largely depends on the modernization of infrastructure. India's borders are vast and varied, covering diverse terrains such as mountains, rivers, and deserts. Therefore, deploying cutting-edge technology is essential. Advanced surveillance technology, including drones, high-resolution cameras, and thermal imaging devices, is crucial for monitoring and securing these extensive borders. Drones equipped with high-definition cameras offer aerial surveillance and real-time data, particularly useful in remote areas. Similarly, the installation of high-resolution cameras, thermal imaging devices, and motion sensors along the borders helps detect unauthorized movements. These technologies capture detailed images and provide alerts for unusual activities. Integrating these technologies into an Integrated Border Management System (IBMS) ensures a centralized approach to monitoring. The IBMS combines satellite imagery, ground sensor data, and human intelligence to create a comprehensive view of border activities, facilitating immediate responses to security threats.

In addition to technology, a well-equipped and trained border security force is essential. Recruitment drives should focus on increasing the number of personnel, while training programs must cover advanced techniques in border management, counter-terrorism, and emergency response. Training should also include the use of modern technology and equipment. Border security forces need to be equipped with state-of-the-art technology, including night vision goggles, communication devices, and all-terrain vehicles, to enhance their efficiency and responsiveness. Regular drills and updates to operational protocols will ensure that these forces are prepared for various scenarios, including breaches, smuggling attempts, and other security incidents.

Physical barriers, such as fences, play a critical role in preventing unauthorized crossings. Existing barriers should be reinforced with additional security layers, such as barbed wire, electronic sensors, and infrared detectors, to increase their effectiveness. In areas where no fencing currently exists, new barriers should be constructed with features designed to withstand various breach attempts, such as anti-climb mechanisms and alarm systems. Regular maintenance and upgrades of these physical barriers are necessary to ensure their continued effectiveness, including inspecting for damage, repairing wear and tear, and incorporating new technological advancements.

2. Tightening Visa Regulations

To prevent the misuse of the visa system, it is crucial to streamline and digitize the visa issuance process. Implementing biometric verification, such as fingerprint and iris scanning, will improve the accuracy of identity checks and help prevent identity fraud. Comprehensive background checks should be conducted for all visa applicants, verifying criminal records, financial stability, and the applicant's ties to their home country. Collaborating with international agencies can provide additional information and verification. The visa application process should be transparent, with clear guidelines and requirements communicated to applicants. An online application system can simplify the process and reduce opportunities for corruption and inefficiency.

A robust visa tracking system is essential for monitoring visa holders. This system should be integrated with national immigration databases to track entry and exit dates, allowing for real-time monitoring and early detection of overstays. Automated alerts should notify authorities of visa overstays or suspicious activities, facilitating prompt action to address violations. Regular audits of the visa tracking system will help identify and address any issues or vulnerabilities, ensuring the accuracy of data and the system's proper functioning.

Increasing penalties for visa violations is another critical step in tightening visa regulations. Penalties should be clearly defined and communicated to applicants, including fines, deportation, and restrictions on future visa applications. Immigration authorities must enforce these penalties rigorously, involving investigations, prosecutions, and consistent application of penalties. Public awareness campaigns can inform visa holders about the consequences of non-compliance, helping to deter potential violators and promote adherence to visa regulations.

3. Strengthening Enforcement Strategies

Effective enforcement of immigration laws requires coordination between central and local authorities. Central and state agencies should work collaboratively to address illegal immigration, sharing information, coordinating operations, and supporting local enforcement efforts. Regular training and briefings for local authorities on immigration policies and procedures will enhance their ability to handle related issues. Adequate resources should be allocated to local authorities, including access to technology, personnel, and training.

Regular audits and inspections are crucial for identifying and addressing illegal immigration. Audits of businesses, particularly those known for employing undocumented workers, should focus on compliance with labor laws and immigration regulations. Businesses found violating regulations should face penalties, including fines and legal action. Inspections should be conducted systematically and fairly, ensuring equitable treatment of all businesses and verifying employee documentation. Publicizing the outcomes of these audits and inspections can deter other businesses from non-compliance and demonstrate the commitment to enforcing immigration regulations.

Encouraging public participation is also key to effective enforcement. Public awareness campaigns should educate citizens about the impact of illegal immigration and the importance of reporting suspicious activities. Establishing anonymous tip lines and online reporting systems will make it easier for the public to provide information about illegal immigration, with these mechanisms being secure and easily accessible. Community outreach programs can engage local communities, fostering cooperation and encouraging reporting, working with community leaders and organizations to promote awareness and participation.

4. Fostering International Cooperation

Strengthening bilateral agreements with neighboring countries is essential for managing cross-border illegal immigration. These agreements should focus on joint border management efforts, including coordinated patrols, information sharing, and joint operations to enhance the ability to prevent and address illegal immigration. Facilitating the exchange of information related to immigration, such as data on known smugglers and illegal immigration trends, helps both countries respond more effectively to emerging threats. Regular meetings between officials from neighboring countries will allow for discussions on border security issues and the coordination of responses, addressing challenges and aligning approaches.

Collaboration with international organizations provides valuable support for immigration management. Organizations such as the UNHCR and IOM offer technical expertise and best practices in immigration management. Leveraging their knowledge and resources can enhance India's immigration policies and practices. Additionally, international organizations may provide funding for projects related to border security and immigration management, which India should seek to support its efforts. Participation in global forums and conferences on migration allows India to stay updated on international trends and policies, facilitating the adoption of effective strategies and practices.

Active participation in regional initiatives is also crucial for addressing illegal immigration. India should contribute to regional security frameworks that address migration and border security issues, collaborating with neighboring countries on joint initiatives and operations. Regional initiatives should also focus on addressing the root causes of migration, such as poverty and conflict, by promoting economic development and stability in source countries. Regional cooperation allows for the sharing of best practices and experiences in managing immigration, leading to the development of effective strategies and solutions.

5. Addressing Root Causes

Promoting economic development in source countries is essential for reducing the push factors of illegal immigration. Supporting education and job creation in these countries provides opportunities and reduces the need for illegal migration. Investment in infrastructure and development projects contributes to stability and growth. India can partner with international organizations to support development programs in source countries, leveraging their resources and expertise. Bilateral aid can also be provided to support economic development and poverty alleviation in source countries, targeting areas that will have the greatest impact on reducing migration pressures.

Enhancing humanitarian assistance can help stabilize regions affected by crises. Providing aid and relief to areas impacted by conflict, natural disasters, and other emergencies reduces the incentive for illegal migration. This support includes assisting refugee camps, providing food and medical aid, and rebuilding infrastructure. Collaboration with international organizations and other countries ensures that aid is effectively distributed and meets the needs of affected populations. Humanitarian assistance should also focus on long-term solutions, such as supporting the rebuilding of communities and promoting economic recovery to prevent future migration pressures.

Aligning immigration policies with international development goals can address broader migration factors. India should align its policies with Sustainable Development Goals (SDGs) related to poverty reduction, education, and economic growth. Supporting these goals will help address the root causes of illegal migration. Participation in global initiatives aimed at addressing migration and development issues will contribute to a coordinated and effective approach, supporting international efforts to promote stability and development in source countries.

Conclusion

Combating illegal immigration requires a comprehensive and coordinated approach that addresses border control, visa regulations, enforcement strategies, international cooperation, and root causes of migration. By implementing the strategies outlined in this chapter, India can strengthen its immigration management, enhance national security, and uphold legal and social standards. Addressing the root causes of illegal migration, such as economic instability and humanitarian crises, will further support these efforts, ensuring a balanced and effective approach to immigration policy. The successful implementation of this multi-layered strategy will not only address the immediate challenges of illegal immigration but also contribute to long-term solutions, creating a more secure and prosperous future for India and its neighbors.

CHAPTER SEVENTEEN

REALITY OF THE WAQF ACT IN INDIA

What is Waqf?

The word "Waqf" originates from the Arabic term "Waqafa," which means the money or goods donated by Muslims for Islamic purposes. In Islamic law, a Waqf is an endowment made by a Muslim for charitable or religious activities, and the property designated as Waqf is meant to be held in perpetuity, remaining inalienable and non-transferable. This concept has its roots in the time of the Prophet Muhammad and was later introduced to India by Islamic rulers during the Delhi Sultanate and Mughal era. These rulers not only brought the idea of Waqf but also implemented it on a large scale, sometimes by converting non-Muslim properties into Waqf assets. Managed by Mutawwalis, or caretakers, who were overseen by Qazis, the system of Waqf was deeply embedded in the Islamic governance structure. This framework was sometimes used to exert religious influence, with Sufis playing a significant role in conversion campaigns, Despite facing challenges during the British Raj, the Waqf system was validated by the British with the Waqf Validating Act of 1913, ensuring its continued existence and influence in Indian society.

The History of Waqf Boards

The institution of Waqf in India has deep historical roots, dating back to the early days of the Delhi Sultanate. It is recorded that Sultan Muizuddin Sam Ghaor dedicated two villages to the Jama Masjid of Multan, entrusting their administration to Shaikhul Islam. As Islamic dynasties, including the Delhi Sultanate, grew in power and influence, the number of Waqf properties across India expanded significantly.

Challenges During the British Era

The late 19th century saw a significant challenge to the existence of Waqf in India. A dispute over a Waqf property reached the Privy Council in London, which was then the highest court of appeal for British India. The British judges presiding over the case criticized the concept of Waqf, describing it as "a perpetuity of the worst and the most pernicious kind," and ultimately declared Waqf as invalid. However, this decision did not sit well in India. The Mussalman Waqf Validating Act of 1913 was introduced to protect the institution, ensuring the continuation of Waqfs in the country. Since then, Waqfs have not only persisted but have also thrived, especially post-independence.

Post-Independence Developments

After India gained independence, the Waqf institution continued to grow, significantly influenced by political factors. The Waqf Act of 1954, passed during Nehru's government, laid the groundwork for the centralization of Waqfs. This led to the establishment of the Central Waqf Council of India in 1964, a statutory body responsible for overseeing the activities of various state Waqf boards, which were established under the provisions of Section 9(1) of the Waqf Act, 1954.

The Waqf Act of 1995 further strengthened the institution, providing comprehensive guidelines for the roles and responsibilities of the Waqf Council, State Waqf Boards, and the Chief Executive Officer. This Act also defined the powers and limitations of Waqf Tribunals, which are empowered to act as civil courts within their jurisdiction. These Tribunals are granted the authority to make binding decisions, which cannot be challenged in any civil court, thus making their rulings final.

The Perpetuity of Waqf Properties

One of the unique aspects of Waqf is that once a property is endowed as Waqf, its ownership is considered to be transferred to Allah, and it remains Waqf property in perpetuity. This principle has led to numerous legal and social disputes over property ownership. A prominent example is the Bengaluru Eidgah ground, where, despite no official title transfer to a Muslim organization, the property was claimed as Waqf based on its status from the 1850s, thus rendering it permanently Waqf property.

Recent Controversies and Claims

In recent years, Waqf Boards have made several controversial claims on various properties. For instance, the Gujarat Waqf Board claimed ownership of the Surat Municipal Corporation building, arguing that it was originally a sarai during the Mughal era, and due to outdated documents, it became Waqf property after independence. The Board's assertion is based on the principle that "once a Waqf, always a Waqf."

Another notable case involves the Gujarat Waqf Board's claim on two islands in Bet Dwarka, located in Devbhoomi Dwarka. The claim, brought before the Gujarat High Court, was met with confusion by the judge, who questioned the legitimacy of Waqf's claim over land in such a historically significant Hindu religious site.

Moreover, the Waqf institution allows for properties to be converted into religious sites without input from others. A striking example occurred in Surat's Shiv Shakti society, where a plot owner registered his property with the Gujarat Waqf Board, transforming it into a holy place for Muslims, much to the surprise of other residents.

Author's views,

The existence of a special Act that governs the religious properties of only one religion in a secular nation like India is deeply problematic and raises serious questions about discrimination. This selective legal protection for Waqf properties, when no equivalent exists for other religious communities, challenges the very principles of equality enshrined in our

Constitution. The ongoing Public Interest Litigation (PIL) in the Delhi High Court by Advocate Ashwini Kumar Upadhyay, which questions the constitutional validity of Waqf, is a timely and necessary examination of this issue. The court's notice to the central government indicates that these concerns are being taken seriously, as they should be.

Moreover, it is worth noting that many Islamic countries, including Turkey, Libya, Egypt, Sudan, Lebanon, Syria, Jordan, Tunisia, and Iraq, do not even have the institution of Waqf. Yet, in India, a nation supposedly committed to secularism, Waqf Boards have become the largest urban landowners, fortified by an Act that legally shields them from challenge. This situation is not only an affront to the secular fabric of our country but also a direct violation of fundamental rights.

As an Indian citizen, I believe this Act must be abolished completely. The notion that Waqf properties are beyond the reach of Indian courts is unacceptable and undermines the rule of law. Every citizen should have the right to challenge the status of Waqf properties in the courts of India, ensuring that no religious group is given preferential treatment over others.

Furthermore, the presence of a law that specifically protects Waqf properties while leaving other religious communities without similar safeguards is a stark example of legal inequality. This selective application of legal protection breeds resentment and divides society. It also perpetuates a system where certain properties are immune from public scrutiny and legal accountability, leading to potential misuse and injustice.

In conclusion, the Waqf Act stands as a clear violation of the principles of equality and secularism that India prides itself on. Its abolition is not only necessary to uphold the Constitution but also to ensure that all citizens, regardless of their religion, are treated with equal respect and dignity under the law. The ability to challenge Waqf properties in Indian courts is a fundamental right that must be restored to safeguard the interests of all Indians.

CHAPTER EIGHTEEN

CHANGE NEEDED IN INDIA'S NUCLEAR POLICY

Story of Nuclear weapons in India

Homi Bhabha, often hailed as the "father of India's nuclear program," played a pivotal role in persuading Jawaharlal Nehru to initiate India's nuclear journey, emphasizing its importance for the nation's energy needs. Initially, both Nehru and Bhabha envisioned the nuclear program as a peaceful endeavor focused on energy rather than weapons development. However, the 1962 war with China exposed India's military vulnerabilities, altering Bhabha's views and underscoring the need for nuclear weapons as a deterrent. This shift in perspective was further solidified when China conducted its first nuclear test in 1964, prompting Bhabha to assert that India could follow suit within 18 months. Although it took a decade for India to conduct its first nuclear test, the foundations for a nuclear weapons program were laid, especially as tensions with Pakistan escalated, leading to Pakistan's commitment to develop its own nuclear arsenal. After the 1965 war, Prime Minister Lal Bahadur Shastri authorized the development of nuclear weapons as a deterrence against both China and Pakistan, a stance later maintained by Indira Gandhi. In 1974, India conducted its first nuclear test, codenamed "Smiling Buddha," signaling its potential nuclear capability. This test, conducted during the Cold War, drew international sanctions, notably from the US, Canada, and Japan. In response, Pakistan sought China's assistance, leading to a secret agreement for nuclear collaboration. Despite ongoing international pressure, India continued to advance its nuclear capabilities, culminating in the 1998 Pokhran-II tests under Prime Minister Atal Bihari Vajpayee, which established India as a nuclear weapons state. These tests defied international norms and led to further sanctions, yet within a decade, the US reversed its stance, signing a civil nuclear deal with India. This marked a significant shift in global perceptions of India's nuclear ambitions. India's nuclear policy, formalized in 2003, emphasizes "No First Use," a doctrine rooted in Nehru's belief in the catastrophic consequences of nuclear warfare and the importance of using nuclear weapons solely as a deterrent, a principle upheld by successive Indian leaders.

The Nation's policy is to have minimum deterrence and credibility.

In a speech, Atal Bihari Vajpayee said "It has been our nation's policy to have minimum deterrence with credibility". Let me break down the idea of "Credible Minimum Deterrence" in simple terms. This policy is about having just enough nuclear weapons to make sure that no one would dare to attack you. The term has three important parts. First, "deterrence" means making the other side think twice before they act. The word "minimum" means keeping only a small number of nuclear weapons, not a huge stockpile. Think of it like this: if your neighbor wanted to break into your house, you wouldn't need a lot of different weapons to stop them. Just one or two guns would likely be enough to make them think it's not worth the risk. This is how India approaches its nuclear policy—having just enough weapons to keep threats at bay, without going overboard, which also saves money.

The last part, "credible," is about being believable. For India's policy to work, it needs to meet three conditions. First, even if someone strikes India first, India must have enough weapons left to hit back. Second, India must be able to reliably deliver these weapons to their targets so that they work as intended. Third, India needs to convince others that it would actually use these weapons if necessary. If all these things are true, then India has a Credible Minimum Deterrence policy.

Author's View,

In my view, while India should always ensure that it remains a responsible nuclear power, it's crucial to put the nation's interests first, especially in dealing with different adversaries. The current 'No First Use' policy works well against a smaller military power like Pakistan, but it might not be as effective against a much stronger power like China. Over the past five decades, China's economy and military have grown significantly, giving them the capability to outmaneuver India's military without needing to resort to nuclear weapons. Since India has committed to using nuclear weapons only if attacked first, this could embolden China to violate India's territorial sovereignty without fearing nuclear retaliation. Security expert Bharat Karnad even suggests that this is why China is acting so aggressively in Ladakh.

Some experts argue that India should consider adopting a more ambiguous nuclear policy, similar to Pakistan's, where the possibility of using nuclear weapons isn't ruled out even if India hasn't been attacked first. They propose a strategy called "escalating to de-escalate," where India would respond to a military threat from China by threatening nuclear retaliation. This approach is intended to make China reconsider any aggressive actions, thereby preventing an attack through the threat of serious retaliation.

However, it's important to recognize that this strategy should be tailored to specific adversaries. For instance, Pakistan's nuclear policy states that it will only use nuclear weapons in the face of a grave existential threat. If India were to adopt an ambiguous nuclear stance towards Pakistan, it could lead to a dangerous escalation. In a situation where tensions rise, Pakistan might feel compelled to use nuclear weapons preemptively, fearing that India might strike first. This is why I believe it's crucial for India to maintain its 'No First Use' policy when dealing with Pakistan, as it helps to prevent unnecessary escalation. But with China, adopting an ambiguous nuclear policy could better safeguard India's national interests.

GOVERNMENT'S ROLE IN VICTIM & WITNESS PROTECTION

The pursuit of justice is the cornerstone of any civilized society. However, the effectiveness of the judicial system hinges not only on the laws in place but also on the safety and security of those who participate in the process—specifically, victims and witnesses. Without adequate protection, victims and witnesses may be reluctant or even unwilling to testify, jeopardizing the integrity of the legal system and allowing criminals to escape justice. This chapter explores the importance of victim and witness protection, why it is urgently needed in India, and how a robust protection plan should be designed and implemented.

What is Victim & Witness Protection?

Victim and witness protection refers to the legal and procedural measures that governments and legal systems put in place to ensure the safety, well-being, and anonymity of individuals who provide crucial testimony in criminal cases. Protection programs can include various elements such as physical security, relocation, identity changes, and financial support. The aim is to protect these individuals from intimidation, threats, or harm that might arise due to their involvement in legal proceedings.

The protection process begins from the moment an individual agrees to testify and continues until the threat is deemed to have subsided. In many cases, it extends beyond the courtroom, ensuring that individuals are safe in their daily lives. This protection is crucial not just for the individuals involved, but also for the judicial system as a whole, ensuring that justice can be served without fear of reprisal.

Why There is a Need for Victim and Witness Protection in India

India's legal system, though comprehensive, has seen numerous instances where the absence of adequate victim and witness protection has led to severe consequences. One of the most tragic and high-profile cases highlighting this need is the murder of key witnesses in the infamous Sohrabuddin Sheikh encounter case.

In this case, Sohrabu**n Sheikh, an alleged gangster, and his wife Kau**r Bi were killed in a police encounter in 2005. The case took a dark turn when Tul**ram Prajapati, a witness to the killings, was also killed in a subsequent encounter, which was later found to be staged. Despite being under government protection, Prajapati's death raised serious concerns about the efficacy of the witness protection mechanisms in place at the time. The case drew national attention, leading to the arrest of several high-profile individuals, including police officers and politicians. However, the murder of key witnesses like Prajapati highlighted the vulnerabilities in the system, where even those under protection were not safe.

Such incidents underscore the dire need for a comprehensive and effective witness protection program in India. The lack of safety not only deters individuals from coming forward but also undermines public confidence in the justice system.

How a New Witness Protection Act Should Be Designed and Implemented

The design of a new witness protection act must be holistic, addressing both the immediate and long-term needs of victims and witnesses. The following are key elements that should be incorporated into the legislation:

1. **Comprehensive Risk Assessment:** The first step in any protection plan should be a thorough risk assessment to identify the level of threat faced by the witness or victim. This would involve evaluating the nature of the crime, the profile of the accused, and any previous threats or attempts to harm the witness. Based on this assessment, a tailored protection plan can be developed.

2. **Physical Protection and Relocation:** For those at high risk, physical protection is paramount. This could include round-the-clock security, safe houses, and, in extreme cases, relocation to a different city or state. The government should also consider the establishment of a dedicated unit within the police force, trained specifically for witness protection duties.

3. **Anonymity and Identity Protection:** In cases where the threat is severe, the government should provide measures to protect the identity of witnesses. This could involve issuing new identity documents, changing names, and providing financial assistance to help the witness rebuild their life under a new identity. The use of technology, such as voice and face modification during court proceedings, can also help protect anonymity.

4. **Legal and Financial Support:** Witnesses often face significant financial and legal challenges as a result of their participation in criminal cases. The new act should include provisions for financial compensation, legal aid, and psychological counseling. This would ensure that witnesses are not left vulnerable or disadvantaged due to their involvement in the justice system.

5. **Special Courts and Fast-Track Trials:** To minimize the time witnesses are at risk, the act should provide for fast-track trials, especially in cases where the lives of witnesses are at stake. Special courts with enhanced security measures should be established to hear such cases, ensuring that

justice is served swiftly and safely.

6. **Strict Penalties for Intimidation or Harm**: The act must also include strict penalties for any attempt to intimidate, threaten, or harm witnesses or their families. Law enforcement agencies should be empowered to act swiftly against anyone found guilty of such offenses, sending a strong message that witness protection is a priority.

7. **Continuous Monitoring and Review**: Even after a trial has concluded, the government should continue to monitor the safety of witnesses for as long as necessary. Regular reviews of the protection program should be conducted to ensure its effectiveness and to make any necessary adjustments.

Implementation Strategy

The successful implementation of a witness protection program requires coordination across various branches of government and law enforcement. The following steps outline how this could be achieved:

1. **Establishment of a National Witness Protection Authority**: A central body should be created to oversee the implementation of witness protection programs across the country. This authority would be responsible for the development of protocols, training of law enforcement, and allocation of resources.

2. **Training and Capacity Building**: Law enforcement officers and judicial staff should be trained specifically in witness protection. This would include understanding the psychological needs of witnesses, methods of protection, and the legal framework surrounding witness protection.

3. **Public Awareness Campaigns**: To build confidence in the new system, the government should launch public awareness campaigns. These campaigns would educate citizens on their rights as witnesses, the protections available to them, and the importance of their role in the justice system.

4. **Monitoring and Accountability**: A robust system of monitoring and accountability should be established to ensure that the protection programs are being implemented effectively. This could involve regular audits, feedback mechanisms, and an independent body to investigate any failures in the system.

5. **Pilot Programs and Phased Implementation**: Before nationwide implementation, the government could roll out pilot programs in selected regions. These pilots would allow for the identification of potential challenges and the refinement of the protection measures before a broader rollout.

Conclusion

In a country as vast and diverse as India, the protection of victims and witnesses is not just a legal necessity but a moral imperative. The failure to safeguard those who come forward to seek justice weakens the very fabric of our society. By implementing a comprehensive witness protection plan, the government can restore faith in the judicial system, ensuring that justice is not only done but seen to be done. The lessons learned from past failures, like the Sohrabuddin Sheikh case, must guide the development of a robust, responsive, and effective witness protection program—one that guarantees the safety of all who seek to uphold the truth. The future of India's justice system depends on it.

CHAPTER TWENTY

RECORDING IN PUBLIC AND PRIVATE SPACES

In an era defined by rapid technological advancements, the need for transparency in every facet of public life has never been greater. The power to hold individuals and institutions accountable, whether in government offices, private enterprises, or public spaces, is integral to fostering a system that truly works for the people. I firmly believe that the government should allow, and even encourage, recording—whether audio or video—in all government offices, public spaces, private stores, and any environment within the public domain. This is not just a proposal for greater transparency; it is a call for a structural shift toward empowering citizens and ensuring accountability at every level.

The Case for Transparency

At the core of any democracy is the idea that power flows from the people. Government officials, public servants, and private businesses providing public services operate within a realm that directly affects the lives of citizens. However, there are numerous cases where individuals experience corruption, harassment, malpractice, or inefficiency in government offices and public services but lack the evidence to bring these issues to light. Allowing recordings in these spaces would provide a tangible solution to this problem, giving citizens the tools to capture instances of wrongdoing and inefficiency.

The Right to Information Act (RTI) revolutionized transparency by allowing citizens to access government records. But RTI has its limitations—it primarily deals with written documents and bureaucratic processes. My proposal is an extension of this right, a Right to Record, empowering people to capture real-time instances of corruption, bias, or incompetence as they unfold. This would make those in positions of power more accountable and deter them from engaging in unlawful activities.

Protecting Public Interest

Take a simple example: an individual visits a government office to get a document processed. They are asked for a bribe to expedite the service. Without the ability to record the conversation, their case becomes a matter of "he said, she said," and the corrupt official can easily evade responsibility. Recording such instances would provide irrefutable evidence, encouraging a more ethical and transparent approach in public offices.

Similarly, in private stores or businesses operating in the public domain, there have been cases of consumer exploitation, price manipulation, and harassment. Giving citizens the right to record these environments ensures that consumers are protected, and businesses are incentivized to maintain high standards of service and fairness.

Why This Proposal Should Be Embraced

One of the arguments against allowing recording in these spaces is privacy concerns. However, we must remember that the right to privacy pertains primarily to personal life, not public duties or interactions that directly affect the public. In government offices or private enterprises serving the public, individuals are acting in a professional capacity. When they perform duties that affect the common man, those actions should be open to scrutiny. Transparency is not an infringement of privacy but a safeguard against misuse of power.

Moreover, with advancements in data protection laws, measures can be introduced to ensure that recordings are used responsibly. For instance, restrictions can be imposed on what can be recorded and how the data can be used. These safeguards would prevent the misuse of recordings while ensuring that the public's right to know is protected.

Addressing Concerns

Critics might argue that allowing citizens to record everywhere could disrupt normal operations or lead to a culture of excessive surveillance. However, this concern can be mitigated by setting clear guidelines on where and when recording is permissible. For example, recording could be restricted to areas where public transactions and services are taking place—such as counters in government offices, service desks in stores, or official meetings. Private discussions unrelated to public services can remain off-limits.

Additionally, the presence of recordings can act as a deterrent for both sides. Citizens will be less likely to falsely accuse officials, knowing that the record will show the truth, while officials and business owners will be more cautious in their dealings, aware that they are being monitored. This balanced approach can create an environment of mutual respect and trust, where transparency becomes the norm, not the exception.

The Role of Technology

The world is rapidly becoming more digital, and smartphones with cameras are ubiquitous. Every citizen already has the tools to record audio and video. It is the legal framework that needs to catch up. Government initiatives that provide easy access to justice, like online complaint portals, can be complemented with the ability to upload recordings directly, ensuring that evidence is reviewed quickly and efficiently.

Introducing this legal right will also drive the development of better technological solutions. Dedicated apps could be developed to allow recordings to be timestamped, encrypted, and stored securely. This would protect the integrity of the evidence, ensuring that recordings are not tampered with or misused.

Impact on Governance and Society

Implementing a policy that allows recordings in government offices and public spaces will serve as a game changer. Government officials will be more cautious and professional in their conduct, knowing that every interaction could be recorded. Corruption will be significantly reduced, as officials will no longer be able to engage in illicit activities without fear of being caught on tape.

For businesses, this move will build greater consumer trust. Companies that operate transparently and treat their customers fairly will have nothing to fear. Instead, they will benefit from increased consumer confidence, as shoppers will feel assured that any malpractice or exploitation will be caught and punished.

Ultimately, a transparent environment fosters greater accountability, efficiency, and trust, which is essential for the overall well-being of society.

Conclusion

By allowing recordings in government offices, private stores, and public spaces, we empower citizens to hold power to account. This proposal is not just about using technology for the sake of it; it's about building a system where transparency is embedded in the very fabric of governance and public life. When every citizen has the power to record, the fear of exposure will act as a natural check on corruption, incompetence, and exploitation.

This initiative aligns with the vision of a progressive Bharat—one that prioritizes the welfare of its citizens, embraces technology to advance its systems, and creates a transparent, accountable, and just society. Let us move forward with the understanding that public service is a public right, and in the age of information, transparency is the foundation of trust.

CHAPTER TWENTY-ONE

Reforms Needed In Education System

In today's rapidly evolving world, the state of our education system is more critical than ever. As we stand at the crossroads of tradition and modernity, addressing the challenges that impede our educational progress is imperative. While foundational to national development, our education system faces significant issues such as inequality, outdated curricula, and inadequate teacher support. As the Minister of Education, I recognize the urgent need for reform to ensure that every student, regardless of their background, has access to quality education that prepares them for the future. This chapter outlines the current problems and proposes innovative solutions to create an education system that not only meets the demands of today but also paves the way for a brighter, more equitable future for all. Although there are many problems I have tried to cover only those which I propose to have a solution to.

Problem 1: Common Board Exams

The Indian education system has long been criticized for its overemphasis on rote learning, particularly in the context of common board exams. These exams, which students face at crucial stages of their academic journey, are designed to test their knowledge across a standardized curriculum. However, the reality is that these exams often encourage students to memorize vast amounts of information without truly understanding the underlying concepts. The pressure to perform well in these exams is immense, leading to a culture where students focus on short-term memorization rather than long-term learning.

This issue is compounded by the fact that the results of these exams play a significant role in determining a student's future opportunities, including college admissions and career prospects. As a result, students often prioritize exam preparation over genuine learning, spending countless hours cramming information rather than engaging with the material in a meaningful way. This not only stifles creativity and critical thinking but also creates a stressful and unhealthy learning environment. Furthermore, the uniform nature of these exams fails to account for individual differences in learning styles, interests, and abilities, leading to a one-size-fits-all approach that does not serve the diverse needs of students.

A solution according to Varad Tikam

To address this deep-seated issue, significant reform is necessary. I propose the elimination of common board exams in favor of entrance exams that are tailored to a student's chosen field of study. Entrance exams should focus on assessing a student's aptitude, critical thinking, and passion for the subject rather than their ability to memorize and regurgitate information. These exams would allow students to demonstrate their understanding of the material in a way that aligns with their future academic and career goals.

For instance, a student interested in pursuing engineering should be tested on their problem-solving abilities, logical reasoning, and understanding of fundamental concepts in physics and mathematics, rather than being required to memorize historical dates or literature summaries. Similarly, a student with a passion for the arts should be evaluated based on their creativity, artistic expression, and understanding of cultural contexts.

By aligning the evaluation process with students' interests and strengths, we can create a more personalized and meaningful education system that encourages deep learning and fosters a lifelong love of learning.

Implementation Plan

1. **Curriculum Development:** The first step in implementing this solution is to develop specialized curricula that cater to different fields of study. This would involve a collaborative effort between educators, industry experts, and academic institutions to create comprehensive and targeted curricula that align with the entrance exams.
2. **Exam Design:** Once the curricula are in place, the next step is to design entrance exams that accurately assess students' knowledge, skills, and aptitude in their chosen fields. These exams should be developed by experts in each discipline and should include a variety of question formats, such as multiple-choice questions, essays, and practical assessments, to evaluate different aspects of a student's abilities.
3. **Teacher Training:** Teachers will need to be trained to adapt to the new curricula and to help students prepare for the entrance exams. This training should focus on promoting critical thinking, problem-solving, and creativity in the classroom, rather than rote memorization.
4. **Pilot Programs:** Before implementing the new system nationwide, pilot programs should be conducted in select schools and regions to test the effectiveness of the new entrance exams and curricula. These pilot programs will provide valuable feedback and allow for any necessary adjustments before full-scale implementation.
5. **Phased Implementation:** The transition to the new system should be gradual, with students in lower grades being introduced to the new curricula and entrance exams first. This phased approach will ensure that students, teachers, and schools have time to adjust to the changes and that any issues can be addressed before the system is rolled out nationwide.
6. **Support and Resources:** To ensure the success of the new system, it is essential to provide students, teachers, and schools with the necessary support and resources. This could include access to study materials, tutoring services, and online platforms that offer practice exams and additional learning opportunities.

7. **Continuous Evaluation:** Finally, the new system should be continuously evaluated to ensure that it is meeting its goals of promoting deep learning and reducing the emphasis on rote memorization. Regular assessments and feedback from students, teachers, and parents should be used to make any necessary improvements to the system.

Problem 2: Caste-Based Reservation

The caste-based reservation system in India was originally implemented to address historical injustices and provide opportunities for marginalized communities. However, over time, this system has become a source of division and controversy. The reservation system, which allocates a certain percentage of seats in educational institutions and government jobs to members of specific castes, has often been criticized for perpetuating social divisions and failing to truly uplift those in need.

One of the primary issues with caste-based reservation is that it often benefits those who are already relatively well-off within their communities, rather than those who are truly disadvantaged. This has led to a situation where merit is sometimes overlooked in favor of caste, leading to resentment among those who feel they are being unfairly excluded from opportunities. Furthermore, the reservation system can create a sense of dependency and entitlement, rather than encouraging self-reliance and hard work.

The current system also fails to address the needs of economically disadvantaged individuals who do not belong to the reserved castes. These individuals often face significant barriers to education and employment, yet they are not eligible for the same opportunities as those from reserved castes. This has led to calls for a more equitable system that takes into account both merit and economic background.

A solution according to Varad Tikam

To create a more just and equitable system, I propose replacing caste-based reservation with a system that is based on merit and economic background. This would involve allocating opportunities based on a combination of academic performance and financial need, rather than solely on caste. By doing so, we can ensure that those who are truly in need of support receive it, regardless of their caste.

Under this new system, students from economically disadvantaged backgrounds would be given priority for scholarships, admissions, and other opportunities, provided they meet certain academic criteria. This approach would reward hard work and achievement, while still providing support to those who need it most. It would also reduce social divisions and promote a sense of unity and fairness within the education system.

Implementation Plan

1. **Policy Reform:** The first step in implementing this solution is to reform existing policies to eliminate caste-based reservation and replace it with a system based on merit and economic background. This will require legislative action and support from both the government and educational institutions.
2. **Data Collection:** To ensure that the new system is effective, it is essential to collect accurate data on students' academic performance and economic background. This data should be used to determine eligibility for scholarships, admissions, and other opportunities.
3. **Scholarship Programs:** New scholarship programs should be established to provide financial support to students from economically disadvantaged backgrounds who demonstrate academic excellence. These programs should be designed to ensure that students have the resources they need to succeed in their studies.
4. **Awareness Campaigns:** To promote the new system and ensure that students and parents are aware of the changes, awareness campaigns should be conducted in schools, communities, and through the media. These campaigns should explain the benefits of the new system and how it works, as well as provide information on how to apply for scholarships and other opportunities.
5. **Monitoring and Evaluation:** The new system should be closely monitored and evaluated to ensure that it is meeting its goals of promoting equity and fairness. This could involve regular assessments of the impact of the new system on students from different economic backgrounds, as well as feedback from students, parents, and educators.
6. **Support for Transition:** To ensure a smooth transition to the new system, support should be provided to students who are currently

benefiting from caste-based reservation. This could include additional tutoring, mentoring, and counseling services to help them adjust to the new criteria and continue to succeed in their studies.

Problem 3: Lack of Genuine Creativity in Projects

In the Indian education system, school and college projects are intended to foster creativity, problem-solving skills, and independent thinking among students. However, in practice, these projects often fail to achieve their intended purpose. A common issue is that many students rely heavily on their parents or external help to complete their projects. This is especially true in younger grades, where parents may feel the need to assist their children to ensure they receive good grades.

This practice undermines the educational value of projects, as the work submitted does not accurately reflect the student's abilities or understanding. Instead of developing creativity and critical thinking, students may learn to rely on others to complete their assignments. This not only hinders their intellectual growth but also leads to a skewed assessment of their abilities. Moreover, the competitive nature of these projects can place undue pressure on students and parents alike, leading to stress and anxiety.

In addition to these issues, take-home projects can also exacerbate inequalities among students. Those with more resources, such as access to better materials or parental support, may produce higher-quality projects, while students from less privileged backgrounds may struggle to compete. This creates an uneven playing field and can lead to feelings of inadequacy and frustration among students who are unable to produce work that meets the same standard.

A solution according to Varad Tikam

To address these issues and ensure that projects truly reflect students' abilities, I propose that all project work be completed within the school or college premises. By conducting projects in a supervised environment, we can ensure that the work produced is entirely the student's own, providing a more accurate assessment of their skills and knowledge. This approach will also foster a greater sense of responsibility and independence among students, as they will be required to manage their time and resources effectively to complete their projects within the allotted time.

Moreover, in-class projects will help level the playing field by ensuring that all students have access to the same materials and resources. This will reduce the impact of socioeconomic disparities on project quality and provide a more equitable learning environment. Teachers will also be able to offer immediate feedback and guidance, helping students to develop their ideas and improve their work in real time.

Implementation Plan

1. **Infrastructure Development:** Schools and colleges must first ensure that they have the necessary infrastructure to support in-class project work. This includes providing adequate space, materials, and equipment for students to complete their projects.
2. **Scheduling:** Schools and colleges should allocate specific times during the school day for students to work on their projects. This could be done during designated project periods or integrated into regular class time, depending on the nature of the project and the subject being taught.
3. **Teacher Training:** Teachers should be trained to facilitate in-class projects effectively. This includes providing guidance on how to encourage creativity and independent thinking, as well as how to assess students' work fairly and consistently.
4. **Resource Allocation:** Schools and colleges should ensure that all students have access to the materials and resources they need to complete their projects. This could include providing basic supplies, access to libraries and research materials, and the use of technology and equipment.
5. **Assessment and Feedback:** Teachers should be encouraged to provide ongoing feedback and assessment throughout the project process. This will help students to develop their ideas, refine their work, and learn from their mistakes, ultimately leading to higher-quality projects.
6. **Parental Involvement:** Schools and colleges should communicate with parents to explain the benefits of in-class projects and encourage them to support their children's independence. Parents should be reassured that the focus is on learning and creativity, rather than producing a perfect final product.

7. **Evaluation and Adjustment:** The implementation of in-class projects should be evaluated regularly to ensure that it is meeting its goals. Feedback from students, teachers, and parents should be used to make any necessary adjustments to the process.

This approach will be used for each problem identified, ensuring that each issue is thoroughly examined and that practical, effective solutions are provided. Let me know if you would like to proceed with all the problems in this format or if you have any specific focus areas.

Problem 4: Imbalanced Student-to-Teacher Ratio

One of the most pressing issues in the Indian education system is the high student-to-teacher ratio, which often far exceeds the ideal ratio of 20:1. In many schools, particularly in rural and government institutions, a single teacher may be responsible for managing classrooms with 40, 50, or even more students. This imbalance places an enormous burden on teachers, who are expected to deliver personalized instruction, manage classroom behavior, and ensure that all students are keeping up with the curriculum.

The consequences of this imbalance are severe. Teachers, overwhelmed by the sheer number of students, are often unable to give individual attention to those who need it most. As a result, many students, particularly those who struggle academically, fall through the cracks. The lack of personalized instruction can lead to lower academic achievement, decreased student engagement, and a higher likelihood of students dropping out. Furthermore, overworked teachers are more likely to experience burnout, leading to higher turnover rates and further exacerbating the problem.

The situation is particularly dire in under-resourced schools, where the shortage of teachers is most acute. In these schools, the high student-to-teacher ratio can severely limit the quality of education that students receive, perpetuating cycles of poverty and disadvantage. The imbalance also hampers the ability of teachers to implement innovative teaching methods or engage in professional development, as they are too preoccupied with managing large classrooms to focus on improving their own skills.

A solution according to Varad Tikam

To address this issue, it is essential to reduce the student-to-teacher ratio to a maximum of 20:1. This ratio is widely recognized as ideal for fostering a productive learning environment where teachers can provide individualized attention and support to each student. By achieving this ratio, we can ensure that all students receive the guidance they need to succeed academically, while also reducing the workload on teachers and improving their job satisfaction.

A lower student-to-teacher ratio will enable teachers to identify and address the unique needs of each student, whether they require additional help with certain subjects or are ready to take on more advanced material. This personalized approach will help to close achievement gaps, boost student confidence, and promote a love of learning. Furthermore, smaller class sizes will create a more manageable and less stressful teaching environment, allowing teachers to focus on delivering high-quality instruction rather than merely maintaining order.

Implementation Plan

1. **Hiring Additional Teachers:** The first and most critical step in reducing the student-to-teacher ratio is to hire more teachers. This will require a significant investment in education, particularly in terms of recruiting and training new educators. The government should prioritize funding for teacher recruitment programs, particularly in under-resourced areas, and offer incentives to attract qualified candidates to the profession.

2. **Teacher Training Programs:** Alongside recruitment, it is essential to provide comprehensive training programs for new and existing teachers. These programs should focus on effective classroom management, personalized instruction techniques, and innovative teaching methods. By equipping teachers with the skills they need to manage smaller classes effectively, we can ensure that the benefits of a reduced student-to-teacher ratio are fully realized.

3. **Infrastructure Expansion:** To accommodate smaller class sizes, schools may need to expand their physical infrastructure, including building additional classrooms and facilities. This will require a coordinated effort between the government, local authorities, and educational institutions

to ensure that the necessary resources are available.

4. **Revising Classroom Assignments:** Schools should review their current classroom assignments and make necessary adjustments to ensure that the new student-to-teacher ratio is implemented across all grades and subjects. This may involve reassigning students and teachers, as well as revising class schedules to accommodate the new structure.

5. **Monitoring and Evaluation:** Once the new ratio is implemented, it is important to monitor its impact on student achievement and teacher satisfaction. Regular assessments should be conducted to evaluate the effectiveness of the smaller class sizes and to identify any areas where further improvements are needed. Feedback from students, teachers, and parents should be used to refine the implementation process and ensure that the benefits of the new ratio are being fully realized.

6. **Sustaining the Ratio:** Maintaining the 20:1 ratio will require ongoing efforts to recruit and retain qualified teachers, as well as continuous investment in educational infrastructure. The government should establish a long-term plan for sustaining the ratio, including provisions for addressing teacher shortages, particularly in rural and underserved areas. Regular audits should be conducted to ensure that schools are adhering to the ratio and that any emerging challenges are promptly addressed.

Problem 5: Neglect of Vedic Science in Modern Education

India has a rich heritage of scientific knowledge that dates back thousands of years. The Vedas, ancient Indian scriptures, contain insights into astronomy, mathematics, medicine, and various other fields that were far ahead of their time. However, much of this knowledge has been forgotten or overlooked in the modern education system, which tends to prioritize Western scientific paradigms. As a result, students are often unaware of India's contributions to global knowledge and are disconnected from their cultural heritage.

This disconnect is problematic for several reasons. Firstly, it undermines national pride and cultural identity, as students are not exposed to the rich intellectual traditions of their own country. Secondly, it represents a missed opportunity to integrate valuable insights from Vedic science into modern scientific research and education. Many principles found in the

Vedas, such as the concept of the atom, the speed of light, and advanced surgical techniques, are now recognized as scientific truths. Yet, these discoveries are often attributed to Western scientists rather than their Indian origins.

Furthermore, the exclusion of Vedic science from the curriculum contributes to a narrow understanding of science among students. It perpetuates the idea that science is a purely Western domain, rather than a universal pursuit that has been enriched by contributions from various cultures, including India. This narrow perspective limits students' appreciation of the diversity of scientific thought and stifles their ability to think critically and creatively about scientific problems.

A solution according to Varad Tikam

To address this issue, I propose the integration of Vedic science into the modern science curriculum. This integration should not be seen as a replacement for Western scientific knowledge but rather as a complementary approach that enriches students' understanding of science as a global and historical endeavor. By studying both Vedic and modern science, students will gain a more holistic understanding of scientific principles and develop a greater appreciation for the contributions of different cultures to the advancement of knowledge.

The integration should focus on areas where there is clear overlap or alignment between Vedic knowledge and modern scientific concepts. For example, the Vedic understanding of the atom, the speed of light, and advanced mathematical techniques should be taught alongside their modern counterparts. Similarly, the principles of Ayurveda, India's traditional system of medicine, can be integrated with modern medical science to provide students with a broader perspective on health and healing.

In addition to the scientific content, the integration should also include discussions on the philosophical underpinnings of Vedic science, such as the emphasis on observation, experimentation, and the pursuit of truth. These discussions will help students to see the connections between ancient and modern scientific methodologies and encourage them to think critically about the nature of scientific inquiry.

Implementation Plan

1. **Curriculum Development:** The first step in implementing this solution is to develop a curriculum that integrates Vedic science with modern science. This will require collaboration between educators, historians of science, and scholars of Vedic literature. The curriculum should be designed to highlight the connections between Vedic and modern scientific concepts and should include both theoretical and practical components.

2. **Teacher Training:** Teachers will need specialized training to effectively teach the integrated curriculum. This training should focus on providing teachers with a deep understanding of Vedic science and its relevance to modern scientific concepts. It should also equip teachers with the skills to engage students in discussions about the philosophical and cultural dimensions of science.

3. **Textbook Revision:** Existing science textbooks should be revised to include content on Vedic science. These revisions should be carefully crafted to ensure that the material is presented in a way that is accessible and engaging for students. The textbooks should include explanations of Vedic concepts alongside modern scientific explanations, as well as case studies and examples that illustrate the practical applications of Vedic knowledge.

4. **Pilot Programs:** Before rolling out the integrated curriculum nationwide, pilot programs should be conducted in select schools to test the effectiveness of the new approach. These pilot programs will provide valuable feedback and allow for adjustments to be made before full-scale implementation.

5. **Assessment Methods:** New assessment methods should be developed to evaluate students' understanding of both Vedic and modern science. These assessments should test students' ability to think critically and creatively about scientific problems, as well as their knowledge of specific scientific concepts. The assessments should be designed to encourage students to see the connections between different scientific traditions and to appreciate the diversity of scientific thought.

6. **Public Awareness Campaign:** A public awareness campaign should be launched to promote the integration of Vedic science into the modern science curriculum. This campaign should highlight the benefits of the integration, such as the enrichment of students' scientific understanding and the promotion of national pride. The campaign should also address any concerns or misconceptions about the integration, emphasizing that

it is not a rejection of modern science but rather an enhancement of it.

7. **Continuous Evaluation:** The integrated curriculum should be continuously evaluated to ensure that it is meeting its goals. Feedback from students, teachers, and parents should be used to make any necessary adjustments to the curriculum, teacher training programs, and assessment methods. Regular reviews should also be conducted to ensure that the curriculum remains up-to-date with the latest scientific research and scholarship on Vedic science.

Problem 6: Lack of Emphasis on Sports as a Career

In India, sports are often viewed as extracurricular activities rather than viable career options. This perception is deeply ingrained in society, where academic achievement is often prioritized over physical education. As a result, many talented young athletes are discouraged from pursuing sports as a career, either by their families, teachers, or societal expectations. This lack of emphasis on sports as a career is compounded by the limited infrastructure and resources available for sports education and training in schools.

The problem is further exacerbated by the lack of professional opportunities for athletes in India. While cricket enjoys immense popularity and support, other sports often struggle to gain the same level of recognition and investment. This disparity limits the opportunities for young athletes to pursue careers in sports other than cricket, leading to a narrow and competitive environment where only a few can succeed.

Moreover, the education system does not adequately support students who wish to pursue sports as a career. Schools often lack the facilities, coaching staff, and time in the curriculum to provide proper sports training. Students who excel in sports may find it difficult to balance their athletic pursuits with their academic responsibilities, leading to burnout or the abandonment of sports altogether. The societal pressure to prioritize academics over sports further limits the opportunities for young athletes to pursue their passion.

The solution according to Varad Tikam

To address this issue, it is essential to promote sports as a viable career option and to provide students with the necessary support to pursue their athletic ambitions. This will require a fundamental shift in societal attitudes towards sports, as well as significant investments in sports infrastructure, training, and education.

One of the key steps in promoting sports as a career is to integrate sports education into the regular school curriculum. This means dedicating specific time each day to physical education and sports training, as well as providing students with access to professional coaching and state-of-the-art facilities. Schools should also offer specialized programs for students who show exceptional talent in sports, allowing them to pursue their athletic goals while still receiving a quality education.

In addition to curriculum changes, there should be greater investment in professional sports leagues and organizations, particularly for sports that are currently underrepresented in India. This will create more opportunities for young athletes to pursue careers in a variety of sports, rather than being limited to a few popular options. The government and private sector should work together to provide funding, sponsorships, and scholarships for young athletes, helping to alleviate the financial barriers that often prevent talented individuals from pursuing sports careers.

Implementation Plan

1. **Curriculum Integration:** Schools should integrate sports education into the daily curriculum, ensuring that students have regular access to physical education and sports training. This will require schools to allocate time each day for sports activities, as well as to invest in the necessary facilities and equipment. Specialized programs should be developed for students who demonstrate exceptional talent in sports, allowing them to pursue their athletic goals alongside their academic studies.

2. **Professional Coaching:** Schools should hire professional coaches to provide high-quality training and guidance to students. These coaches should be experienced in their respective sports and should be able to help students develop their skills, set goals, and prepare for competitions. Schools should also establish partnerships with local sports clubs and organizations to provide additional training and

resources for students.

3. **Sports Infrastructure:** The government should invest in the development of sports infrastructure in schools, particularly in under-resourced areas. This includes building sports facilities such as stadiums, courts, and tracks, as well as providing equipment and materials for a variety of sports. The government should also work with private sector partners to fund the construction of sports facilities and to provide sponsorships and scholarships for young athletes.

4. **Public Awareness Campaign:** A public awareness campaign should be launched to promote the value of sports as a career option. This campaign should highlight the achievements of Indian athletes in various sports and should emphasize the importance of physical fitness, discipline, and teamwork. The campaign should also address societal attitudes towards sports, encouraging families and communities to support young athletes in their pursuit of sports careers.

5. **Professional Opportunities:** The government and private sector should work together to create more professional opportunities for athletes in India. This includes expanding professional leagues for various sports, providing funding and sponsorships for athletes, and establishing partnerships with international sports organizations. The government should also provide financial incentives for companies that support sports development and should offer tax breaks for businesses that invest in sports infrastructure and training programs.

6. **Scholarships and Funding:** Scholarships and funding should be made available to students who wish to pursue sports careers. This will help to alleviate the financial barriers that often prevent talented individuals from pursuing their athletic ambitions. The government should establish a national scholarship program for young athletes, providing financial support for training, travel, and competition expenses. Private sector partners should also be encouraged to contribute to scholarship funds and to sponsor young athletes.

7. **Monitoring and Evaluation:** The implementation of these initiatives should be regularly monitored and evaluated to ensure that they are effective in promoting sports as a career option. Feedback from students, coaches, and schools should be used to make any necessary adjustments to the programs and initiatives. Regular assessments should be conducted to measure the impact of the initiatives on student participation in sports, as well as on the number of students pursuing

sports careers.

Problem 7: Lack of Industry Exposure and Career Guidance in Schools

A significant gap in the Indian education system is the lack of industry exposure and career guidance provided to students. Most students graduate with theoretical knowledge but are often ill-equipped to navigate the complexities of the job market or pursue careers aligned with their skills and interests. The absence of regular interaction with industry professionals and limited opportunities for practical, hands-on experiences leave students unprepared for real-world challenges.

This disconnect between education and industry is particularly concerning given the rapidly changing job landscape. The rise of automation, artificial intelligence, and the gig economy demands a workforce that is adaptable, skilled, and well-informed about emerging career opportunities. However, the traditional education system in India has been slow to adapt to these changes, resulting in a mismatch between the skills taught in schools and those required by employers.

Furthermore, many students are unaware of the full range of career options available to them. They may follow conventional paths due to societal pressures or a lack of exposure to alternative fields. This limited perspective can lead to dissatisfaction and underemployment, as students may end up in careers that do not align with their passions or strengths.

A Solution according to Varad Tikam

To bridge this gap, schools must integrate regular industry engagement and career guidance programs into the curriculum. By bringing industry experts into the classroom and providing students with real-world experiences, we can better prepare them for the demands of the modern job market. These initiatives will also help students make informed decisions about their career paths, ensuring that they pursue fields that align with their interests and abilities.

Regular industry engagement can take various forms, including guest lectures, workshops, internships, and industry visits. These interactions will give students insights into different career options, the skills required in various industries, and the realities of working in different fields. Additionally, schools should establish partnerships with local businesses, startups, and industry organizations to facilitate these engagements and provide students with networking opportunities.

Career guidance programs should be comprehensive and tailored to individual students' needs. They should include assessments of students' strengths, interests, and values, as well as information about different career paths and the educational requirements for each. Guidance counselors should work closely with students to help them set realistic goals and develop action plans to achieve their career aspirations. These programs should also provide support for students who may face challenges in pursuing their desired careers, such as financial barriers or lack of access to resources

Implementation Plan

1. **Establishing Industry Partnerships:** Schools should actively seek partnerships with local businesses, startups, and industry organizations. These partnerships can facilitate guest lectures, workshops, internships, and industry visits, providing students with direct exposure to different career fields. Schools should also collaborate with industry partners to develop curricula that align with current industry needs and trends.
2. **Guest Lectures and Workshops:** Schools should organize monthly guest lectures and workshops led by industry professionals from various fields. These sessions should cover a wide range of topics, including emerging technologies, industry trends, and career development strategies. Students should be encouraged to ask questions and engage in discussions to deepen their understanding of different career options.
3. **Internship Programs:** Schools should offer internship programs that allow students to gain practical experience in their chosen fields. These internships should be available to students in their final years of school and should be structured to provide meaningful, hands-on learning experiences. Schools should work with industry partners to ensure that internships are well-supervised and aligned with students' career interests.
4. **Career Guidance Counseling:** Every school should have trained career guidance counselors who can provide personalized support to students.

These counselors should conduct assessments to help students identify their strengths, interests, and career goals. They should also provide information about different career paths, including the education and skills required for each. Counselors should work with students to develop action plans for achieving their career aspirations and provide support for overcoming any challenges they may face.

5. **Industry Visits:** Schools should organize regular industry visits for students, allowing them to see different work environments and learn about various career fields firsthand. These visits should be planned in collaboration with industry partners and should include opportunities for students to interact with professionals and ask questions about their work.

6. **Career Fairs:** Schools should host annual career fairs where students can meet with representatives from various industries, educational institutions, and training programs. These fairs should provide students with information about different career options, as well as opportunities to network with potential employers and mentors.

7. **Continuous Monitoring and Feedback:** The effectiveness of industry engagement and career guidance programs should be continuously monitored and evaluated. Schools should collect feedback from students, teachers, and industry partners to assess the impact of these initiatives and make any necessary adjustments. Regular reviews should be conducted to ensure that the programs remain relevant to the changing job market and continue to meet the needs of students.

Problem 8: Rigid School Timings and Lack of Flexibility

The traditional school schedule in India, typically from 9 AM to 4 PM, is often rigid and does not accommodate the diverse needs and learning styles of students. This inflexibility can lead to inefficiencies in the learning process, as students may struggle to focus or engage during certain parts of the day. Moreover, the long hours spent in school can contribute to burnout and stress, particularly when combined with the demands of homework, extracurricular activities, and exam preparation.

The current system also fails to account for the fact that different students have different peak performance times. Some students may be more alert and focused in the morning, while others may perform better in the afternoon or evening. The one-size-fits-all approach to school scheduling does not allow for these differences, which can hinder students' ability to learn effectively and achieve their full potential.

Additionally, the rigid school timings can limit students' opportunities to pursue other interests or engage in self-directed learning. With little time available outside of school hours, students may struggle to balance their academic responsibilities with extracurricular activities, hobbies, or part-time work. This lack of flexibility can stifle creativity, reduce motivation, and negatively impact students' overall well-being.

A Solution according to Varad Tikam

To address these issues, schools should adopt more flexible schedules that accommodate the diverse needs of students. This could include offering different start times, shorter school days, or block scheduling, where students focus on fewer subjects each day for longer periods. By providing flexibility in the school schedule, we can create a learning environment that is more conducive to student engagement, motivation, and well-being.

One approach to flexible scheduling is to offer students the option to choose their start time within a certain range, such as between 8 AM and 10 AM. This would allow students to begin their school day at a time that aligns with their natural rhythms and peak performance times. Schools could also implement block scheduling, where students focus on two or three subjects each day for extended periods, rather than juggling multiple subjects in short periods. This approach can reduce the cognitive load on students and allow for deeper, more focused learning.

Another option is to shorten the school day to six hours, with a focus on quality over quantity. By reducing the time spent in school, students will have more time to pursue extracurricular activities, engage in self-directed learning, and take care of their mental and physical health. Schools could also offer flexible attendance options, such as allowing students to work from home on certain days or providing online learning opportunities.

Implementation Plan

1. **Pilot Flexible Scheduling Programs:** Schools should start by piloting flexible scheduling programs in select classes or grades. This will allow

them to test different scheduling models, such as variable start times, block scheduling, or shortened school days. The pilot programs should be carefully monitored to assess their impact on student engagement, academic performance, and well-being.

2. **Surveying Student and Parent Preferences:** Before implementing flexible scheduling on a larger scale, schools should survey students and parents to understand their preferences and needs. This feedback will be essential in designing schedules that work for the majority of students and their families.

3. **Staff Training and Support:** Teachers and staff will need training and support to adapt to flexible scheduling models. This may include professional development on managing longer class periods, differentiating instruction, and using technology to facilitate online learning. Schools should also provide resources and support for teachers to help them adjust to the new schedules.

4. **Infrastructure and Technology:** Schools may need to invest in infrastructure and technology to support flexible scheduling. This could include upgrading classroom facilities to accommodate longer periods, providing students with access to online learning platforms, and ensuring that all students have access to the necessary technology at home.

5. **Flexible Attendance Policies:** Schools should consider implementing flexible attendance policies that allow students to work from home on certain days or to attend classes online. These policies should be designed to accommodate students' individual needs while ensuring that they continue to receive a quality education.

6. **Continuous Monitoring and Adjustment:** As with any major change, the implementation of flexible scheduling should be continuously monitored and adjusted as needed. Schools should collect feedback from students, parents, and teachers to identify any challenges or areas for improvement. Regular assessments should be conducted to evaluate the impact of the new schedules on student learning, engagement, and well-being.

Problem 9: Overburdened Teachers and Limited Professional Autonomy

In India, teachers are often confronted with numerous challenges that hinder their effectiveness and job satisfaction. These challenges include excessive workloads, inadequate salaries, and a lack of professional autonomy. Teachers frequently face an overwhelming array of responsibilities, including administrative tasks, non-teaching duties, and stringent regulations, which detract from their primary focus—educating students.

The issue of excessive workloads is a significant concern. Teachers are often required to perform additional duties such as election responsibilities, census counting, and other administrative tasks that are unrelated to their core teaching functions. These extra responsibilities not only consume valuable time but also contribute to high levels of stress and burnout. The cumulative effect of these demands can negatively impact the quality of education that teachers are able to provide.

Salaries for teachers in India are often low, especially when compared to the rising cost of living and the demanding nature of their work. This financial strain can lead to job dissatisfaction and a lack of motivation. Low salaries also discourage talented individuals from entering or remaining in the teaching profession, exacerbating issues of teacher shortages and quality.

Professional autonomy is another area of concern. Teachers are often subject to strict regulations, including dress codes and limitations on their personal expression. This lack of freedom can stifle creativity and diminish job satisfaction. Teachers are also frequently discouraged from participating in public discourse or expressing their opinions on educational policies or other issues. The lack of representation in policy-making processes means that teachers' voices are often not heard, further contributing to their sense of marginalization.

A Solution according to Varad Tikam

To address these issues, a comprehensive approach is needed that focuses on enhancing teacher support, improving compensation, and granting greater professional autonomy. By addressing these areas, we can create a more positive and effective working environment for teachers, ultimately leading to better educational outcomes for students.

Increasing teacher salaries is a fundamental step toward recognizing and rewarding the hard work and dedication of educators. Competitive salaries will not only improve teachers' financial stability but also attract and retain talented individuals in the profession. The government should conduct a thorough review of teacher salaries and implement adjustments to ensure that they are commensurate with the demands of the job and the cost of living.

Reducing non-teaching duties is essential for allowing teachers to focus on their core responsibilities. This can be achieved by delegating administrative tasks to specialized staff or creating support roles within schools. Teachers should not be burdened with additional responsibilities that detract from their primary role of educating students. Schools and government agencies should collaborate to streamline processes and ensure that teachers can dedicate their time and energy to their teaching responsibilities.

Providing professional development opportunities is crucial for supporting teachers' growth and career advancement. Schools should offer regular training programs, workshops, and conferences to help teachers stay current with educational trends and best practices. Additionally, clear pathways for career advancement should be established, allowing teachers to take on leadership roles and contribute to policy development.

Granting teachers greater autonomy in their classrooms is important for fostering a creative and effective learning environment. Teachers should have the freedom to design and implement their own teaching methods and approaches, tailored to the needs of their students. Schools should support teachers' right to express their opinions and participate in public discourse without fear of repercussions.

Implementation Plan

1. **Salary Increases:** The government should conduct a comprehensive review of teacher salaries to ensure they are competitive with other professions. Salary adjustments should be based on experience, qualifications, and the cost of living in different regions. Schools should explore additional compensation options, such as performance-based bonuses or stipends for special achievements.
2. **Reducing Non-Teaching Duties:** Schools and government agencies should work together to minimize the number of non-teaching duties assigned to teachers. This may involve delegating tasks such as election

duty or census counting to other personnel or creating support roles within schools to handle administrative tasks. By reducing non-teaching duties, teachers will have more time to focus on their core responsibilities.

3. **Professional Development Programs:** Schools should establish regular professional development programs for teachers, including workshops, conferences, and training sessions. These programs should cover a range of topics, including new teaching methods, educational technologies, and curriculum development. Schools should provide funding and support for teachers to attend external professional development opportunities.

4. **Career Advancement Opportunities:** Clear pathways for career advancement should be established within the education system. This may include opportunities for teachers to take on leadership roles, such as department heads or curriculum coordinators, as well as opportunities for involvement in policy development and educational research. Schools should work to create a supportive environment for teachers to pursue these opportunities.

5. **Enhanced Autonomy and Freedom:** Teachers should be granted greater autonomy in their classrooms, allowing them to design and implement their own teaching methods and approaches. Schools should also support teachers' right to express their opinions and participate in public discourse without fear of repercussions. This can be achieved by promoting a culture of openness and respect for teachers' professional judgment and contributions.

6. **Regular Monitoring and Feedback:** The effectiveness of these measures should be regularly monitored and evaluated. Schools should collect feedback from teachers to identify any challenges or areas for improvement. Regular assessments should be conducted to measure the impact of the measures on teacher satisfaction, performance, and retention.

By implementing these solutions, we can create a more supportive and effective environment for teachers, ultimately leading to improved educational outcomes for students and a more sustainable education system.

In conclusion, the proposed reforms to the Indian education system aim to address several critical issues that impact its effectiveness and fairness. By shifting from a caste-based reservation system to one that prioritizes merit and economic background, we can create a more equitable and efficient system that better serves students from diverse backgrounds. The emphasis on merit-based reservations ensures that academic excellence is rewarded, while economic background-based reservations target support where it is most needed, addressing the root causes of socio-economic disparity.

Furthermore, the reduction of additional duties for teachers, improved salaries, and enhanced professional development opportunities are essential for fostering a supportive and productive work environment. By addressing these issues, we can improve teacher satisfaction, retention, and overall effectiveness, which in turn benefits students and the education system as a whole.

Implementing robust measures to prevent examination leaks, integrating Vedic science with modern education, and adopting flexible project and exam policies will contribute to a more transparent, innovative, and fair educational process. These reforms not only aim to enhance the quality of education but also to ensure that the system is inclusive and responsive to the needs of all students.

The successful execution of these reforms requires a coordinated effort from policymakers, educators, and the community. By working together to implement these changes, we can build an education system that is not only more equitable and effective but also better aligned with the aspirations and potential of every student. These reforms are a crucial step towards transforming the Indian education system into one that truly reflects merit, supports socio-economic advancement, and prepares students for a dynamic and competitive world.

CHAPTER TWENTY-TWO

PASHUPATINATH ACT

In the heart of our nation, where compassion and reverence for all living beings are deeply rooted in our culture, animals continue to suffer in silence. Whether on the streets, in homes, farms, or the wild, animals face an unimaginable reality of pain, neglect, and exploitation. As custodians of this land, we have a moral duty to protect them. This chapter delves into the ground reality of the problems faced by animals in India, presents possible solutions, and concludes with the drafting of the 'Pashupatinath Act'—a proposed legislation to safeguard their welfare.

The name "Pashupatinath Act" draws inspiration from Pashupatinath, one of the revered forms of Lord Shiva, often regarded as the "Lord of Animals" in Hindu History. The name embodies the deep-rooted cultural and spiritual reverence India holds for all living beings, particularly animals, symbolizing compassion, protection, and care. By invoking Pashupatinath, the Act emphasizes that the responsibility to safeguard the welfare of animals is not just a legal obligation but a moral and spiritual duty, in line with India's ancient tradition of coexistence with nature and all its creatures.

Ground Reality—The Struggles of Animals

Stray Animals: The Voiceless on the Streets

The streets of India teem with millions of stray dogs, cats, and cattle, living in destitute conditions. These animals, often abandoned or born on the streets, battle for survival every day. With no access to clean water, nutritious food, or shelter, they scavenge through trash, struggling to stay alive.

One of the most heartbreaking practices involves separating newborn pups from their mothers. Often, people take away these vulnerable pups shortly after birth to sell or raise them in ways that deprive them of crucial maternal care. This leads to malnourishment, weakened immune systems, and severe developmental problems. These pups, without the nurturing and protection of their mothers, face a higher risk of mortality, diseases, and mistreatment.

Additionally, malnutrition plagues stray animals, leading to weakened immune systems, infections, and life-threatening diseases like rabies. The lack of medical care means even minor wounds become fatal over time. Strays also endure cruelty at the hands of people, who throw stones, poison them, or call municipal authorities for their removal—often in inhumane ways. Traffic accidents claim the lives of countless strays, left to die on the roads without help.

Domestic Animals: Neglected in Homes and Farms

Though domesticated animals like dogs, cats, and livestock live closer to humans, their reality is not much brighter. Many are abandoned by their owners once they grow old, sick, or expensive to care for, joining the stray population on the streets. Even those that remain in homes often suffer from neglect—improper feeding, lack of vaccinations, and minimal medical care. Pets may be kept in cages for long periods, deprived of interaction, exercise, or freedom.

In rural areas, working animals like bullocks, horses, and camels are overworked and underfed, with their injuries ignored. Commercial breeding practices in cities and villages have turned pets into commodities, with female animals suffering repeated pregnancies in unsanitary, cramped conditions.

Wildlife: A Battle Against Extinction

Wild animals, integral to India's ecosystem, face relentless threats. Deforestation has led to habitat destruction, forcing elephants, tigers, and leopards into human settlements in search of food and shelter. The shrinking of forests has caused a rise in human-wildlife conflict, with animals often killed when they stray into villages.

Illegal poaching continues to devastate wildlife populations. Tigers are hunted for their bones, elephants for their tusks, and pangolins for their scales, fueling a dangerous black market. Weak enforcement of wildlife protection laws and corruption have crippled conservation efforts, leaving these magnificent creatures vulnerable to extinction.

Farm and Livestock Animals: The Forgotten Workers

Farm animals like cows, goats, and chickens are essential to rural livelihoods, but their treatment is often brutal. Living in cramped, filthy enclosures, these animals face malnutrition, poor hygiene, and a lack of medical attention. Dairy cows are overmilked, leading to infections, while animals bred for meat are slaughtered in inhumane conditions. The journey to slaughterhouses is harrowing—animals crammed into trucks without food or water, many dying before they reach their destination.

The Scourge of Cruelty and Abuse

Deliberate abuse of animals is rampant. Stray dogs are beaten, tortured, and killed for amusement. Religious and cultural festivals often exploit bulls, horses, and elephants, forcing them to perform in parades and ceremonies without regard for their well-being. Despite laws like the Prevention of Cruelty to Animals Act, enforcement remains weak, with legal loopholes and societal apathy allowing abusers to escape punishment.

Solutions according to Varad Tikam

1. Public Awareness and Education

Raising awareness about animal welfare through public campaigns is the foundation for change. Schools, colleges, and workplaces should educate people about responsible pet ownership, stray animal care, and the importance of wildlife conservation.

2. Stray Animal Management Programs

A structured stray animal management program involving sterilization, vaccination, and community feeding would address the stray population crisis. Municipalities must work alongside NGOs to implement animal birth control (ABC) programs, ensuring humane treatment of strays.

3. Stricter Enforcement of Animal Welfare Laws

Strengthening the enforcement of existing animal welfare laws is crucial. Strict penalties for animal abuse, illegal breeding, and neglect must be imposed. Law enforcement officers need specialized training to handle animal-related cases, and courts should prioritize such cases to set examples.

4. Wildlife Conservation and Anti-Poaching Efforts

Greater investment in protecting wildlife sanctuaries and national parks is needed. Anti-poaching units must be equipped with better resources and training, while international cooperation can help crack down on illegal wildlife trade. Buffer zones around forests should be created to reduce human-wildlife conflicts.

5. Humane Farming Practices

The government should mandate humane farming practices, ensuring livestock are provided with adequate space, nutrition, and medical care. Strict guidelines should regulate transportation and slaughter of farm animals, requiring monitoring to prevent cruelty.

6. Veterinary Care and Animal Shelters

Veterinary services must be expanded, especially in rural areas, to provide treatment for sick and injured animals. The establishment of more animal shelters and sanctuaries would offer abandoned, injured, and elderly animals a safe place to live.

7. National Database for Animal Breeders

A national database should be established for animal breeders to track breeding practices, ensuring ethical treatment of animals. This would help curb illegal breeding and the exploitation of female animals.

8. Ban on Early Separation of Pups from Mothers

A ban on separating young pups from their mothers before they are properly weaned should be enforced nationwide. Separating pups from their mothers too early causes psychological and physical harm to both the mother and the pups. There must be strict punishment for those who engage in this practice.

The Pashupatinath Act, 20XX

To ensure comprehensive protection for animals, the following draft of the 'Pashupatinath Act' is proposed:

Preamble: Recognizing the deep connection between humans and animals and the essential role animals play in our ecosystems, society, and culture, it is the duty of the nation to ensure their protection. This Act aims to establish a legal framework for the welfare, conservation, and humane treatment of animals in India.

Chapter I: Rights and Protection of Animals

1. Right to Life and Freedom from Cruelty All animals, whether stray, domestic, wild, or farm, shall have the right to live free from torture, abuse, and cruelty. Any form of mistreatment, deliberate harm, or neglect will be punishable by law.

2. Right to Adequate Nutrition and Medical Care Animals shall have the right to access proper food, water, and medical care. Owners and caretakers must ensure the provision of basic necessities, and stray animals shall be provided for through community programs.

3. Right to a Safe and Natural Habitat Wild animals shall have the right to live in their natural habitats, free from human encroachment. Deforestation and illegal poaching will be treated as serious offenses, and offenders shall face stringent legal consequences.

Chapter II: Regulation and Enforcement

1. Establishment of the Animal Welfare Board An independent 'Animal Welfare Board' shall be established to oversee the implementation of animal protection laws. This board will be responsible for monitoring, enforcing, and advising the government on animal welfare policies.

2. Strengthened Penalties for Cruelty Offenses against animals, including cruelty, illegal poaching, and abuse, shall result in imprisonment for up to 10 years and/or heavy fines, depending on the severity of the offense.

3. Protection of Stray Animals Municipalities are responsible for the humane management of stray animals through sterilization and vaccination programs. The killing of stray animals without just cause will result in severe punishment.

4. Ban on Early Separation of Pups from Mothers It shall be illegal to separate young pups from their mothers before the age of 8 weeks. Violators will face imprisonment for up to 3 years and/or fines as deemed appropriate. This law will ensure the pups' physical and emotional well-being, as well as prevent the psychological harm caused to mother animals due to early separation.

Chapter III: Conservation of Wildlife

1. Preservation of Natural Habitats The government shall take proactive steps to prevent deforestation and the destruction of wildlife habitats. Buffer zones will be established to minimize human-animal conflict.

2. Anti-Poaching and Wildlife Trafficking Measures Anti-poaching efforts shall be intensified, and collaboration with international bodies will be encouraged to stop the illegal wildlife trade. Wildlife reserves will be monitored strictly to prevent any illegal activity.

Chapter IV: Humane Farming and Livestock Practices

1. Ethical Treatment of Farm Animals Livestock and farm animals must be treated humanely, provided with adequate living space, nutrition, and medical care. The transportation and slaughter of animals will be regulated by strict guidelines to ensure humane practices.

2. Monitoring and Accountability of Breeders Breeders must register with the national database and follow ethical breeding practices. Exploiting animals for commercial purposes will lead to immediate suspension of breeding licenses and legal penalties.

Conclusion

The 'Pashupatinath Act' is not just a set of laws but a testament to our responsibility towards the creatures with whom we share this planet. This Act, once implemented, will ensure that animals are no longer silent victims of cruelty, neglect, and exploitation. It is time for us to act with compassion and bring about a legal revolution that secures their future, for a nation that cannot protect its animals can never be truly humane.

Regulation and Enforcement

1. Establishment of the Animal Welfare Board An independent 'Animal Welfare Board' shall be established to oversee the implementation of animal protection laws. This board will be responsible for monitoring, enforcing, and advising the government on animal welfare policies.

2. Strengthened Penalties for Cruelty Offenses against animals, including cruelty, illegal poaching, and abuse, shall result in imprisonment for up to 10 years and/or heavy fines, depending on the severity of the offense.

3. Protection of Stray Animals Municipalities are responsible for the humane management of stray animals through sterilization and vaccination programs. The killing of stray animals without just cause will result in severe punishment.

4. Ban on Early Separation of Pups from Mothers It shall be illegal to separate young pups from their mothers before the age of 8 weeks. Violators will face imprisonment for up to 3 years and/or fines as deemed appropriate. This law will ensure the pups' physical and emotional well-being, as well as prevent the psychological harm caused to mother animals due to early separation.

Chapter III: Conservation of Wildlife

1. Preservation of Natural Habitats The government shall take proactive steps to prevent deforestation and the destruction of wildlife habitats. Buffer zones will be established to minimize human-animal conflict.

2. Anti-Poaching and Wildlife Trafficking Measures Anti-poaching efforts shall be intensified, and collaboration with international bodies will be encouraged to stop the illegal wildlife trade. Wildlife reserves will be monitored strictly to prevent any illegal activity.

Chapter IV: Humane Farming and Livestock Practices

1. Ethical Treatment of Farm Animals Livestock and farm animals must be treated humanely, provided with adequate living space, nutrition, and medical care. The transportation and slaughter of animals will be regulated by strict guidelines to ensure humane practices.

2. Monitoring and Accountability of Breeders Breeders must register with the national database and follow ethical breeding practices. Exploiting animals for commercial purposes will lead to immediate suspension of breeding licenses and legal penalties.

Conclusion

The 'Pashupatinath Act' is not just a set of laws but a testament to our responsibility towards the creatures with whom we share this planet. This Act, once implemented, will ensure that animals are no longer silent victims of cruelty, neglect, and exploitation. It is time for us to act with compassion and bring about a legal revolution that secures their future, for a nation that cannot protect its animals can never be truly humane.

MOTHERLAND OR DEATH

In an era where the safety and integrity of the nation hang by a thread due to growing terrorism, India must take a firm stance. As the name of this chapter suggests, it is not merely a slogan but a policy proposal that defines India's approach towards individuals who dare to challenge the sovereignty and peace of this great land. We must realize that the safety of our Motherland is paramount, and those who jeopardize it should not expect mercy.

India's soft approach in the past, such as returning the body of Burhan Wani, a known terrorist, to his family for a traditional burial, must be re-evaluated. The aftermath of this decision saw large gatherings that glorified Wani's death, turning his funeral into a rallying point for separatist sentiments. This sends a dangerous message — one that paints terrorists as martyrs. The USA, by contrast, handled the death of Osama bin Laden with a firm hand. After eliminating the mastermind behind the 9/11 attacks, the U.S. government ensured that bin Laden's body was buried at sea, erasing the possibility of his grave becoming a shrine for extremists. This level of decisiveness is what India must adopt.

To prevent any glorification of terrorists, India should implement a policy where terrorists' bodies are never returned. Instead, they should be dealt with in a manner that leaves no trace of their existence. This denies extremists any physical focal point for gathering support and eliminates the potential for their legacy to inspire further violence.

Hijackings and Their Cost: A Historical Lesson

India has often found itself forced to negotiate with terrorists due to the safety of innocent lives. A prime example of this is the IC 814 Kandahar hijacking in 1999. Terrorists hijacked an Indian Airlines plane in route from Kathmandu to Delhi and diverted it to Kandahar, Afghanistan. After days of negotiation, India was forced to release three high-profile terrorists, including Masood Azhar, who later became the head of the Jaish-e-Mohammed terrorist group. This incident underlined the high cost of India's perceived leniency towards terrorism. Releasing these terrorists led to further attacks, including the 2001 Parliament attack.

This history cannot be repeated. India must declare that it will no longer negotiate with terrorists, no matter the circumstance. The lives of many more are at stake if a handful of terrorists are freed to continue their mission of violence.

According to Varad Tikam

A New Way to Handle Terrorists: Torture Over Death

When a terrorist is sentenced to death, we must remember the words of Lord Krishna in the Bhagavad Gita, where he tells Ashwatthama that death is not the ultimate punishment, but a form of *mukti* — liberation. Hanging or executing terrorists swiftly offers them an escape. What we need instead is a system where terrorists are made to endure a slow, agonizing process of death — a deterrent that ensures their end is as painful as the chaos they inflict on innocent lives.

Terrorists should face a lifetime of suffering. Psychological and physical torment must replace the death penalty, ensuring that those who engage in acts of terrorism are not granted a quick or easy death. The pain and fear they cause should be mirrored back onto them.

India's Zero Tolerance to Terrorism

We must, as a nation, send a resounding message: there will be no tolerance for terrorism in any form. Whether homegrown or imported, those who seek to destabilize our country will face the harshest possible consequences.

No more will we allow terrorists' bodies to become symbols of martyrdom. No more will we allow planes to be hijacked and terrorists released. No more will India be a land that forgives or forgets when it comes to the security of its people.

"Motherland or death. There is no in-between."

CHAPTER TWENTY-FOUR

PROBLEMS IN INDIAN POLICE

The Indian police force, despite being the backbone of law and order, faces numerous challenges that prevent it from operating at full efficiency. These problems are deeply rooted in administrative shortcomings, systemic issues, and social mistrust, which collectively hinder the ability of law enforcement agencies to maintain peace and enforce justice effectively. This chapter will explore these challenges and present a comprehensive solution plan to overcome them.

Administrative Challenges

1. Overburdened Police Force

The Indian police force is severely overburdened, with the police-to-population ratio standing at just 157 officers per 100,000 people, far below the UN-recommended figure of 222 per 100,000. This shortfall creates immense pressure on the existing force, which is expected to deal with a vast array of duties, including crime prevention, law enforcement, maintaining public order, conducting investigations, and managing traffic.

In many urban areas, where the population is dense, police officers are often required to work long hours without adequate rest, leading to fatigue and mental exhaustion. This workload also diminishes the quality of policing as officers are unable to dedicate sufficient time to investigations and preventive measures. In rural areas, the problem is exacerbated, with police stations often serving multiple villages, making it difficult to respond to emergencies promptly. This not only affects the police's ability to maintain order but also increases stress levels among officers, leading to high rates of burnout and attrition.

2. Weak Infrastructure and Equipment

Another pressing issue is the lack of modern infrastructure and equipment within the police force. Many police stations across the country still rely on outdated tools such as *lathis* (wooden sticks) for crowd control and basic policing. Modern law enforcement requires advanced tools and protective gear to ensure the safety of both police personnel and civilians. Yet, equipment like riot helmets, tactical gas masks, ballistic helmets, bulletproof vests, riot shields, and tasers are often missing.

In riot situations or during mob control, the lack of protective gear makes police officers vulnerable, leading to higher casualties and injuries. Similarly, in high-risk operations, officers lack advanced firearms and tactical gear, which puts them at a significant disadvantage. The absence of personal radios and other communication tools during such operations severely hampers coordination, often leading to delayed responses. This inability to deploy appropriate force in critical situations undermines the effectiveness of the police and leaves them unequipped to deal with modern-day challenges such as terrorism and organized crime.

3. Low Budget Allocation

Despite the increasing demands on the police force, only about 3% of the national budget is allocated to policing. This limited funding severely hampers the operational efficiency of the police, affecting everything from salaries and recruitment to training, infrastructure development, and the acquisition of modern equipment. Underfunded police departments often struggle to maintain basic resources such as police vehicles, firearms, communication equipment, and forensic tools.

The inadequate budget also limits the scope of recruitment, leading to manpower shortages across the country. Police officers frequently have to rely on outdated, inefficient methods due to the lack of funds for research, development, and the adoption of advanced technologies. This underfunding also negatively impacts the welfare of police personnel, with many officers working long hours for relatively low pay, leading to dissatisfaction and further contributing to corruption and inefficiency.

4. Lack of Accountability

One of the major systemic problems in Indian policing is the lack of accountability. While there is a clear hierarchy within the force, it often fails to ensure that officers at all levels are held responsible for their actions. Senior officers, especially those with political connections, can often evade scrutiny, while junior officers bear the brunt of any blame for systemic failures. This culture of passing the blame down the chain of command creates an environment of impunity, particularly for those in positions of power.

This lack of accountability also leads to corruption, with senior officers sometimes using their influence to shield those engaged in illegal activities. The connection between politics and policing is particularly troubling, as it allows for the manipulation of law enforcement to serve personal or political agendas, rather than the interests of justice and public safety. Additionally, this has a demoralizing effect on lower-ranking officers, who may feel disillusioned and powerless within the system, leading to a cycle of inefficiency and corruption.

5. Underreporting of Crime

Another major issue is the underreporting of crime. Often, when citizens approach the police to file a First Information Report (FIR), they are given a blank sheet of paper instead, known as a "white paper," on which they are asked to write their complaint. This informal method bypasses the official FIR process, which would otherwise require the police to open an investigation and report the case to higher authorities.

The reason for this underreporting is that police officers are reluctant to increase their official caseload, as each FIR requires extensive documentation and investigation, adding to their already overwhelming workload. This practice leads to a significant underestimation of the crime rate, preventing the true scale of crime from being addressed. It also prevents victims from receiving timely justice, as many cases go unrecorded and, therefore, uninvestigated.

Social Challenges

1. Trust Deficit

One of the most significant social challenges faced by the Indian police is the trust deficit between the police and the public. Many people view the police with suspicion, associating them with corruption, brutality, and inefficiency. This perception is fueled by frequent reports of police misconduct, including instances of custodial torture, bribery, and unnecessary harassment. As a result, citizens are often reluctant to approach the police, even when they are in need of help.

This trust deficit has far-reaching consequences, as it weakens the relationship between law enforcement and the communities they are meant to serve. Without the cooperation and support of the public, police efforts to maintain law and order are severely hampered. The lack of trust also creates a reluctance to report crimes, as many people believe the police will either fail to act or may themselves be complicit in wrongdoing.

2. Political Interference

Political interference is another major factor that undermines the independence and integrity of the police force. In India, it is common for politicians to use the police to further their own agendas, whether by suppressing dissent, protecting political allies, or targeting opposition figures. This interference not only compromises the neutrality of the police but also leads to selective enforcement of the law.

In many cases, political leaders influence the appointment and promotion of senior police officers, ensuring that those loyal to them hold positions of power. This creates a conflict of interest, as these officers may prioritize political loyalty over their duty to uphold the law. It also results in the police being used as a tool for political vendettas, rather than as a service focused on public welfare.

3. Inadequate Training

Training is a crucial aspect of law enforcement, and unfortunately, the Indian police force is often inadequately trained to meet the demands of modern policing. The training programs currently in place are often outdated and fail to provide officers with the necessary skills to handle the complexities of issues such as cybercrime, terrorism, and human rights violations.

Moreover, there is little emphasis on specialized training for officers tasked with handling sensitive situations such as gender-based violence or crimes against children. The lack of proper training also impacts the investigative capabilities of the police, leading to poorly conducted investigations, mishandling of evidence, and delayed justice. Without regular and updated training, the police force struggles to keep pace with the evolving nature of crime, especially in the digital age.

Solutions according to Varad Tikam

To address the multitude of problems faced by the Indian police force, a comprehensive and multi-faceted reform plan is required. Below are detailed solutions to each of the major challenges identified:

1. Increase in Police Manpower

The first and most immediate step to relieve the burden on the police force is to increase recruitment. The government should initiate continuous recruitment drives to increase the police-to-population ratio to at least meet the UN-recommended figure of 222 officers per 100,000 people. Additionally, special units should be established to handle specific types of crime, such as cybercrime, terrorism, and organized crime, ensuring that officers with specialized skills are available where they are most needed.

2. Modernization of Infrastructure and Equipment

The police force must be equipped with modern infrastructure and the latest technology. This includes providing officers with advanced protective gear such as ballistic helmets, vests, and riot shields, as well as communication tools like personal radios and mobile forensic labs. In addition, police stations should be modernized with state-of-the-art computer systems, forensic tools, and surveillance equipment, allowing officers to respond more effectively to crimes and emergencies.

3. Higher Budget Allocation

The budget allocated to the police must be increased substantially from the current 3% to at least 5-6%, with a focus on improving personnel salaries, increasing recruitment, and providing modern equipment. A larger budget will also allow for better training facilities, welfare schemes for police personnel, and the adoption of new technology. These resources will empower the police to perform their duties more effectively, increasing overall public safety and reducing crime rates.

4. Enhanced Accountability Mechanisms

To improve accountability, an independent police oversight commission should be established, with the authority to investigate complaints against police officers and ensure that all ranks are held responsible for their actions. This body should be free from political influence and should focus on upholding the law impartially. Additionally, regular performance reviews should be conducted to evaluate the effectiveness of officers, with clear consequences for those who fail to meet standards of conduct and duty.

5. Reform in Crime Reporting

To address the issue of underreporting, the government should implement a digital FIR filing system, which allows citizens to lodge complaints online. This system would automatically generate an official record, ensuring that all cases are documented and investigated. Furthermore, police stations should be required to publicly display the number of FIRs filed each month, increasing transparency and accountability.

Conclusion

Policing in India, though essential to maintaining law and order, faces severe administrative, infrastructural, and social challenges. These problems undermine the effectiveness of the police force, reducing public trust and enabling crime to persist unchecked. Comprehensive reforms are required to modernize the police force, equip officers with the necessary tools and training, and ensure that law enforcement operates independently and fairly. By addressing these issues head-on, India can build a police force that is efficient, transparent, and trusted by the people. Only then can the country move towards a safer and more just society.

CHAPTER TWENTY-FIVE

TAX EXEMPTION FOR ESSENTIAL PROFESSIONS

In every society, certain professions form the backbone of its progress, security, and well-being. Teachers mold the future generations, police officers maintain law and order, farmers ensure the nation is fed, doctors save lives, emergency responders provide critical assistance in times of crisis, and the defense forces protect our borders and sovereignty. These are not just jobs; they are vocations that involve immense dedication, often at the cost of personal comfort and security. Yet, these professionals, who contribute directly to the well-being and future of the nation, often find themselves burdened by the same tax obligations as those in far less essential sectors. I propose that a select group of professions—particularly teachers, police, agricultural workers, doctors, emergency services, and members of the defense forces—should be exempt from paying taxes. This policy change would not only recognize their critical contributions but also serve as a powerful incentive for others to join these fields, ensuring a stronger and more stable nation.

The Case for Teachers

Teachers are the architects of the nation's future. They shape the minds and values of the next generation, ensuring that society continues to progress in knowledge, ethics, and innovation. Despite their central role, teachers in India often face low salaries, excessive workloads, and limited opportunities for growth. The current tax system further diminishes their already meager take-home pay, leaving them struggling to make ends meet.

By exempting teachers from taxes, the government would acknowledge their importance to the nation's long-term growth. This policy would also help attract more talent to the teaching profession, which is currently facing a shortage of qualified and motivated educators. With higher net income, teachers would be able to invest more in their own education and resources, enhancing the quality of education they provide. Ultimately, a nation that invests in its educators is a nation that invests in its future.

The Case for Police

Police officers are the unsung heroes who maintain peace, order, and security in our society. They risk their lives daily to protect citizens from crime, violence, and unrest. Despite their vital role, the police force in India is often underfunded, overworked, and underappreciated. Officers face dangerous working conditions, long hours, and constant public scrutiny. Yet, their salaries are modest, and the tax burden further reduces their ability to support their families.

Exempting police officers from taxes would not only improve their quality of life but also boost morale within the force. When officers feel that their government truly values their sacrifices, they are more likely to perform their duties with dedication and pride. A tax exemption would also help alleviate some of the stress associated with their job, leading to better decision-making and higher levels of public trust in law enforcement.

The Case for Doctors and Healthcare Workers

Doctors and healthcare professionals serve as the frontline defense against disease, injury, and pandemics. Their contributions to society, especially during global health crises like COVID-19, are immeasurable. Yet, despite their life-saving work, doctors often face high levels of stress, long working hours, and enormous responsibilities, all while shouldering significant financial burdens, including taxes. Many doctors in rural areas also work for minimal pay, driven more by their dedication to service than monetary rewards.

A tax exemption for doctors and healthcare workers would acknowledge their pivotal role in safeguarding the nation's health. It would allow them to focus more on their mission of healing without the added strain of heavy taxation. Furthermore, such a policy could incentivize more healthcare professionals to serve in underdeveloped regions, addressing the ongoing shortage of medical professionals in rural India.

The Case for Emergency Responders

Emergency services, including firefighters, paramedics, and disaster relief workers, are vital during times of crisis. These individuals rush into dangerous situations to save lives, provide critical medical attention, and offer essential relief to affected communities. Whether responding to natural disasters, accidents, or emergencies, they perform selfless acts that are often underappreciated.

By offering tax exemptions to emergency responders, the government would recognize the life-saving role these professionals play in society. It would also provide a financial cushion for individuals who face high levels of physical and emotional stress in their line of work. This would ultimately help improve emergency response capabilities, as more people would be drawn to these noble yet demanding professions.

The Case for Farmers and Agricultural Workers

Agriculture is the lifeblood of India, providing food security and employment to a large portion of the population. Farmers work tirelessly, often under harsh conditions, to ensure that the country is fed. Yet, despite their critical role, farmers face numerous challenges, including unpredictable weather, fluctuating market prices, and limited access to modern technology. These challenges are compounded by the fact that many farmers earn barely enough to sustain themselves and their families.

While India already provides some financial relief to farmers, including subsidies and loan waivers, a tax exemption for agricultural workers would go a step further in securing their livelihoods. Such a policy would not only protect farmers from financial distress but also encourage the younger generation to remain in or return to farming. The agricultural sector, which is the backbone of the Indian economy, deserves this recognition and support.

The Case for the Defense Forces

Members of the defense forces stand at the frontline of the nation's security, safeguarding its borders and protecting its sovereignty. Their work involves immense risk, with many soldiers sacrificing their lives for the country. Despite the high risks and demands of military life, many defense personnel are paid modest salaries and subjected to taxes that reduce their financial stability.

Exempting defense personnel from taxes is not just a financial incentive; it is a moral responsibility. Soldiers and officers dedicate their lives to the protection of the country, and the least the nation can do is ease their financial burden. A tax exemption would also serve as a gesture of gratitude from the nation, recognizing the sacrifices they make daily to ensure the safety and security of its citizens. This policy would improve morale within the armed forces and act as a powerful recruitment tool, ensuring that India continues to have a strong and capable military force.

According to Varad Tikam

Supporting Economic Growth

Critics may argue that offering tax exemptions to these professions could lead to a loss in government revenue. However, the long-term benefits of such a policy far outweigh any short-term losses. By offering tax relief to teachers, police officers, farmers, doctors, emergency responders, and defense personnel, the government would strengthen the very foundations of society.

For instance, a better-compensated teaching force would produce a more educated and innovative population, leading to higher productivity and economic growth. Similarly, a better-supported police force would ensure greater social stability, which is essential for economic development. A financially secure farming community would lead to higher agricultural output, lower food prices, and greater food security. Doctors and emergency responders, relieved of the financial burden of taxes, would continue saving lives and ensuring the nation's health and safety. Lastly, defense personnel, with the financial relief of tax exemption, would remain focused and dedicated to their duty of protecting the nation.

A Moral Responsibility

Beyond the economic argument, there is a moral imperative to support those who dedicate their lives to serving the nation. Teachers, police officers, farmers, doctors, emergency responders, and defense personnel all contribute to the public good in ways that are not always reflected in their paychecks. They perform services that are essential to the functioning of society, and it is only fair that the government recognizes this through tax exemptions.

By lifting the tax burden from these professions, we would be acknowledging their sacrifices and contributions. This policy would send a powerful message that the government values those who put the nation's needs above their own and is willing to take concrete steps to support them. It would also encourage others to follow in their footsteps, ensuring that these essential professions are filled with talented and motivated individuals.

Conclusion

The proposal to exempt certain professions from taxes is not merely a financial policy; it is a step toward social equity. Teachers, police officers, farmers, doctors, emergency responders, and members of the defense forces are the pillars of our society, and they deserve to be treated with the respect and support that reflects their contributions. By implementing tax exemptions for these essential professions, the government would be investing in the nation's future, ensuring that the foundations of education, health, security, and agriculture remain strong and resilient.

This policy would also help bridge the gap between the rich and the poor, as those in these professions often belong to the lower and middle-income groups. Tax relief would provide them with much-needed financial stability, allowing them to live with dignity and continue their vital work for the nation. A tax-free system for these essential professions is not just a reward—it is a recognition of their critical role in building and sustaining the nation.

VEHICLE SURVEILLANCE SYSTEM

In today's fast-paced world, technology is rapidly evolving, and its integration into our daily lives is more prevalent than ever. One area where technology can have a profound impact is in the realm of public safety, law enforcement, and transparency. I propose that every vehicle in Bharat—be it cars, bikes, scooters, or trucks—should be mandated to have both a front dashcam and a rear camera installed. These cameras should record continuously, and the footage must be stored both on a physical drive within the vehicle and on a secure government web server.

This proposal aims to create a nationwide network of vehicular surveillance that can assist law enforcement agencies in solving crimes, help reduce traffic violations, and generally enhance safety on the roads.

The Vision

Imagine a Bharat where every vehicle, from the congested streets of Mumbai to the serene lanes of rural villages, is part of a vast surveillance network. These dashcams and rear cameras would function as an interconnected web, capturing events in real time and storing the footage both locally and in the cloud. This footage could then be accessed by authorities to assist in criminal investigations, traffic disputes, and insurance claims, and even to monitor potential threats to national security.

Such a system would also act as a deterrent to reckless driving, hit-and-run cases, and road rage incidents, as individuals would be conscious of the fact that they are being monitored.

Government-Driven Manufacturing Mandate

To ensure the seamless implementation of this system, the government must collaborate with vehicle manufacturers across Bharat. A legal mandate would be established, requiring all automobile manufacturers—whether domestic or international operating in Bharat—to install both a front dashcam and a rear camera in every vehicle produced, starting from a specified date.

This mandate would apply to all vehicles: cars, bikes, scooters, trucks, and public transport. By making this feature standard in every vehicle, the government can ensure uniformity, reliability, and accountability. Vehicle manufacturers would be responsible for integrating these cameras into their vehicles during production, ensuring compliance with government standards for resolution, storage, and security.

The costs of these devices would be absorbed into the overall price of the vehicles, but with economies of scale, the financial impact on consumers would be minimal. In return, drivers would gain added protection and the assurance of enhanced security on the roads.

Benefits of the System

1.

Crime Prevention and Investigation

- One of the most significant advantages of a vehicle surveillance system is the ability to quickly gather evidence. Imagine a scenario where a crime is committed, and a getaway vehicle is used. With cameras installed in every vehicle on the road, authorities can immediately trace the route taken by the criminal by accessing the video footage from surrounding vehicles. This could be vital in tracking criminals or even locating stolen vehicles.
- Moreover, crimes like abductions, assaults, and thefts could be captured in real-time, providing investigators with concrete evidence. In many cases today, authorities are forced to rely on grainy CCTV footage from a handful of cameras, but with this system, they would have access to multiple angles, improving the chances of solving the crime.

2.

Reducing Traffic Violations

- A constant surveillance network could drastically reduce the number of traffic violations, including speeding, illegal overtaking, running red lights, and reckless driving. By recording all vehicle movements, any violations would be captured on video, and fines could be issued based on indisputable evidence.
- In case of an accident, the footage would be crucial for determining fault and ensuring that insurance claims are processed fairly. This would also discourage false claims or manipulations, which are often seen in insurance fraud cases.

3.

Preventing Hit-and-Run Incidents

- Hit-and-run incidents are notoriously difficult to investigate. Often, the culprits flee the scene, leaving little evidence behind. However, with every vehicle in the vicinity recording at all times, law enforcement could easily track the offending vehicle and hold the driver accountable.

◦ Additionally, the mere presence of such cameras would serve as a deterrent to drivers contemplating fleeing after an accident, as they would know that their escape is being documented by multiple vehicles.

4.

Improved Road Safety

◦ A constant watch on vehicular movements can help ensure better driving discipline. The awareness that every vehicle is recorded will encourage people to follow road rules, respect pedestrian rights, and maintain safe distances from other vehicles. This can lead to a reduction in road accidents and save thousands of lives every year.

◦ For example, drivers would think twice before tailgating, overtaking dangerously, or engaging in road rage, knowing that their behavior is being recorded and could result in heavy penalties.

5.

Assisting in Disaster Management

◦ In the event of natural disasters, this vehicle surveillance system could provide authorities with real-time data on which areas are most affected. Emergency vehicles can then be dispatched more effectively, and authorities could coordinate relief efforts based on real-time traffic conditions and road situations.

◦ In case of accidents or mass emergencies like pile-ups or fires, the footage from nearby vehicles could offer a detailed understanding of the sequence of events and enable quicker resolutions.

6.

Monitoring Public Safety and National Security

- This system could also play a crucial role in combating terrorism and organized crime. In the unfortunate event of terrorist attacks, law enforcement agencies could track vehicles involved, even after they have left the scene. By having a record of the vehicle's movements from all possible angles, authorities could quickly neutralize threats and prevent further harm.
- Similarly, illegal activities such as smuggling and human trafficking, which often rely on vehicular transportation, could be exposed through this network of cameras. With real-time feeds and stored footage, investigative agencies could track suspicious movements and intervene more effectively.

Possible Scenarios Solved with this Implementation

1.

Hit-and-Run Case

- A pedestrian is struck by a speeding car in a busy street in Delhi. The driver speeds off, leaving no clue about his identity. However, thanks to the dashcam footage from other vehicles, authorities can immediately track the route of the fleeing car and identify the license plate. Within hours, the perpetrator is located and arrested. Without this surveillance system, such cases often remain unsolved due to a lack of evidence.

2.

Preventing Insurance Fraud

- A driver deliberately crashes into another car to claim insurance, but the footage from both the victim's car and the vehicles around it show that the crash was staged. The insurance company denies the fraudulent claim, and the fraudster is held accountable for attempting to exploit the system.

3.

Tracking Terrorist Activity

- ○ Intelligence agencies receive a tip-off about a potential terrorist threat in a major city. The suspect is spotted in a vehicle, and using the vehicle surveillance network, authorities are able to trace his movements across different regions. The footage from various vehicles helps pinpoint the terrorist's location, leading to his arrest before the attack can take place.

4.

Solving a Murder Case

- ○ A high-profile assassination takes place in a public area. The criminal escapes in a vehicle, but dashcam footage from surrounding vehicles provides police with a clear view of the escape route, allowing them to track down the perpetrator. Without this system, authorities might have to rely on vague eyewitness reports or fragmented CCTV footage, delaying justice.

5.

Rescue Operations in Disaster Zones

- ○ A severe flood hits a city, leaving roads blocked and traffic stranded. Emergency vehicles rely on real-time feeds from nearby vehicles to understand which areas are accessible and which roads are flooded. This allows them to prioritize rescue operations and provide timely assistance to those in need.

Challenges and Solutions

1.

Privacy Concerns

- A primary concern with such a system would be the invasion of privacy. However, this can be addressed by ensuring that footage is stored securely and can only be accessed by authorized personnel in case of emergencies or crimes. Proper safeguards and encryption methods must be put in place to prevent unauthorized access to the data.

2.

Cost of Implementation

- Installing dashcams and rear cameras in every vehicle might be seen as an expensive mandate. However, the cost can be reduced by allowing private manufacturers to compete in producing affordable, high-quality camera systems. Additionally, the long-term benefits of improved safety, reduced crime, and better traffic management far outweigh the initial investment.

3.

Data Storage and Management

- Storing footage from millions of vehicles on a central server would require a massive infrastructure. To tackle this, a hybrid system can be implemented where short-term data is stored on local drives in the vehicles, while important incidents and flagged footage are uploaded to a central server. This will reduce the burden on cloud storage and ensure efficient use of resources.

Conclusion

In conclusion, mandating dashcams and rear cameras in every vehicle in Bharat and connecting them to a central surveillance network is a powerful solution to many of the country's current challenges, including crime prevention, traffic regulation, and national security. By creating a network of eyes on the road, we can not only improve safety but also foster a sense of accountability among citizens. With vehicle manufacturers working alongside the government to implement these systems, the benefits—ranging from solving hit-and-run cases to tackling terrorism—are far-reaching. It is time we embrace this technological revolution for the betterment of Bharat's future.

 दंड (DAND)

In the age of smartphones and digital tools, Bharat stands on the brink of a major transformation. As we aim to create a nation rooted in transparency, accountability, and justice, there is a pressing need for systems that not only empower law enforcement but also enable the common citizen to participate in safeguarding our country. One such revolutionary tool I propose is दंड **(Dand)**, a government-made app that will allow citizens to anonymously report various crimes, from traffic violations to corruption, tax fraud, and more.

दंड will not only make it easier to report violations, but it will also incentivize civic responsibility by offering rewards to those who help expose wrongdoing. The app, combined with advanced face-recognition software and integration with Bharat's Universal Card system, will serve as a comprehensive mechanism to promote justice and discipline.

The Vision Behind दंड

The name "दंड" is derived from the Sanskrit word for "punishment," symbolizing a tool that brings justice to those who break the law. The vision behind दंड is to ensure that no violation goes unnoticed, no matter how minor, and that citizens can play an active role in maintaining law and order. Imagine a nation where every individual has the power to expose corruption or crime by simply using their smartphone, a tool that most citizens already have in their pockets.

While governments and law enforcement agencies have made great strides in combating crime and corruption, the sheer scale of the problem requires innovative solutions. दंड will act as a bridge between the people and the government, giving ordinary citizens the ability to report violations while receiving rewards for their efforts.

How दंड Will Work

दंड will be a user-friendly app designed for quick reporting and secure submission of evidence. Here's how the app will work:

A. Reporting Violations and Crimes with Evidence

दंड will provide users the ability to report a wide range of violations. Some examples include:

- **Traffic Violations:** Citizens will be able to report instances of reckless driving, parking violations, running red lights, or not following lane discipline. Imagine a scenario where a person is stuck in traffic and notices a car brazenly driving on the wrong side of the road. With दंड, they can snap a picture of the license plate, upload it to the app, and submit it to the authorities within seconds.
- **Corruption and Bribery:** Imagine walking into a government office and witnessing a clerk accepting a bribe for approving documents faster. With दंड, a citizen can secretly record a video or take a photo of the incident and upload it anonymously. The evidence is forwarded to anti-corruption agencies, which can then take swift action.

- **Tax Fraud and Financial Crime:** Often, people are aware of businesses or individuals involved in tax evasion, but fear repercussions for reporting it. दंड will allow anyone to anonymously report instances of tax fraud. For instance, a person who knows of an influential businessperson under-reporting income can submit this information, and if the claim is validated and recovered, they will receive half of the money recovered.
- **Public Nuisance and Littering:** Another common violation is littering and public nuisance. A person walking down the street might witness someone carelessly throwing trash on the road. Through दंड, they can take a picture of the violator, and submit it through the app, and the face recognition technology (discussed later) will help identify the individual for imposing fines.

In each case, the submission is simple: take a picture or video, attach a brief description, and submit it. The system will ensure the report reaches the correct authorities, who will verify the evidence and take action.

B. Anonymity for Safety

To protect citizens from potential backlash, दंड will allow users to report violations **anonymously**. This will be particularly crucial in cases of reporting corruption or financial crimes, where the violator might have the power to intimidate or retaliate against the reporter. Ensuring anonymity will give citizens the confidence to come forward without fear. For those who choose to report with their identity revealed, the app will provide an option to link their report to their Universal Card.

C. Rewards for Reporting

To motivate citizens to actively use दंड, the app will feature a **reward system**. If a report leads to a fine, seizure, or the recovery of money, the citizen who submitted the report will receive 50% of the fine or recovered amount. For example:

- **Traffic Violation:** If a report about a vehicle breaking traffic laws results in a fine of ₹5000, the reporter will receive ₹2500 directly into their account linked to the app.

- **Corruption and Tax Fraud:** If a reported case of corruption leads to a recovered sum of ₹1 lakh, the reporter will receive ₹50,000 as a reward.

This system will ensure that citizens have a personal incentive to act against wrongdoing. It turns every mobile phone user into a guardian of justice, empowering millions to hold violators accountable.

3. Advanced Features of दंड

Integration with Universal Card and Face Recognition Software

The app will integrate with Bharat's **Universal Card system**, a national identity platform proposed in another chapter of this book. The Universal Card will store biometric information, personal details, and a record of an individual's legal and financial history. By integrating the face-recognition software with this Universal Card, दंड will provide an unmatched level of accuracy in identifying violators.

For instance, if someone reports a case of littering, and the video captures the face of the person responsible, the app will automatically match the face with the Universal Card database. This will help authorities issue fines or summonses directly, ensuring that the offender is identified without requiring the person to disclose their identity.

AI-Driven Verification

While encouraging public participation, it's equally important to ensure that the app is not misused for false reporting or framing innocent individuals. To prevent this, दंड will employ **artificial intelligence (AI)** to cross-verify the validity of the submitted evidence. For example, the AI system could analyze the timestamps, location data, and patterns in videos or photos to check if they have been tampered with. It will also cross-check vehicle registration numbers and look for repeat offenders.

Potential Situations Where दंड Could Make a Difference

To understand how impactful दंड can be, let's consider a few real-world scenarios:

Situation 1: A Corrupt Building Inspector

Ravi is a young entrepreneur who's starting his own business. He recently purchased a small plot of land and applied for building permits. However, the building inspector, Mr. Verma, demands a ₹50,000 bribe to approve the paperwork. Ravi, frustrated but afraid of repercussions, quietly records the conversation and uploads it to दंड. His report reaches the anti-corruption bureau, and within a week, Mr. Verma is caught and punished. Ravi also receives a portion of the recovered bribe, helping him financially while bringing a corrupt official to justice.

Situation 2: Traffic Chaos in a Busy City

Pooja is driving to work in one of Bharat's bustling metropolitan cities. At a major intersection, she sees multiple cars jumping red lights, causing a dangerous traffic situation. Frustrated, she pulls out her phone, opens दंड, and takes pictures of the offenders' license plates. Later that day, she receives a notification that her report led to fines for the violators, and she receives ₹3000 as her share of the fines collected. Not only did she make a small profit, but her actions also improved road safety in her community.

Situation 3: A Case of Tax Fraud

Shyam works as an accountant for a medium-sized business. He discovers that his employer has been hiding a portion of the company's earnings to avoid taxes. Knowing that he could face serious consequences for reporting it openly, Shyam uses दंड to submit documents and financial statements as proof. The tax authorities recover ₹20 lakh from the business, and Shyam is rewarded with ₹10 lakh for his bravery and contribution to bringing justice.

Implications of दंड

Empowering Citizens and Strengthening Society

The core mission of दंड is to empower citizens by giving them a direct role in maintaining law and order. When millions of people are involved in monitoring violations, Bharat will become a more disciplined and transparent society. This will result in:

- **Reduction in Traffic Violations:** The fear of being reported will lead to more disciplined drivers on the roads.
- **Reduction in Corruption:** The threat of being recorded or photographed by a vigilant citizen will deter government officials from engaging in corrupt practices.
- **More Efficient Law Enforcement:** Law enforcement agencies will be able to focus their resources on more significant crimes while the public handles smaller violations through reporting.

Fostering Civic Responsibility

By incentivizing reports with rewards, दंड will foster a culture of civic responsibility. Citizens will no longer feel helpless when they witness wrongdoing. Instead, they'll have the power to act, knowing they'll be rewarded not just morally but also financially.

Challenges and Solutions

A. Preventing Misuse

The possibility of false or malicious reporting exists. To counter this, दंड will have a system of verification to ensure that all reports are accurate and valid. Users who repeatedly submit false reports will be penalized or banned from using the app.

B. Protecting Privacy

While the app will use face recognition and the Universal Card for identification, strict privacy measures will be in place to ensure that data is only used for law enforcement purposes. Sensitive information will be encrypted, and access will be restricted to authorized personnel only. Additionally, regular audits will be conducted to ensure compliance with privacy regulations, and citizens will be informed about how their data is being used.

C. Technical and Operational Hurdles

The implementation of दंड will require significant investment in technology and infrastructure. The app must be robust, secure, and capable of handling large volumes of data. To address these challenges:

1. **Infrastructure Development:** The government will partner with leading technology firms to develop a scalable and secure platform. This includes ensuring the app can handle high traffic volumes and integrating it with existing databases and systems.
2. **Training and Capacity Building:** Law enforcement officers and administrative staff will undergo training to efficiently handle and process the reports submitted through दंड. This training will focus on using the app, verifying reports, and maintaining data security.
3. **Public Awareness Campaign:** To ensure the successful adoption of दंड, a nationwide campaign will be launched to educate citizens about the app's features, benefits, and how to use it effectively. This will include workshops, online tutorials, and promotional events.

Potential Impact and Future Prospects

A. Enhanced Accountability

दंड will dramatically enhance accountability across various sectors. With a tool that allows citizens to report and get rewarded for their contributions, there will be a notable reduction in illegal activities and violations. Public officials and businesses will be more cautious, knowing that their actions can be easily documented and reported.

B. Improved Governance

The data collected through दंड will provide valuable insights into patterns of violations and corruption. This data can be used to inform policy decisions, identify systemic issues, and develop targeted interventions. For example, if a particular area is identified as having frequent traffic violations, targeted enforcement strategies can be implemented there.

C. Encouraging Civic Engagement

The app will encourage active civic engagement by showing citizens that their efforts can lead to tangible changes. It will foster a sense of responsibility and involvement in the community. This increased engagement can lead to a more informed and active citizenry, which is crucial for the democratic process.

D. Scaling and Adaptation

The success of दंड in Bharat could serve as a model for other countries grappling with similar issues. The app's technology and approach could be adapted and scaled for use in different contexts, promoting global collaboration in fighting corruption and crime.

Conclusion

दंड represents a transformative approach to governance and civic engagement. By empowering citizens to report crimes and violations, and rewarding them for their contributions, Bharat can foster a culture of transparency, accountability, and civic responsibility. The integration of advanced technologies, such as face recognition and the Universal Card system, will further enhance the app's effectiveness, ensuring that justice is not only served but also witnessed by the public.

In creating दंड, we are not just developing a tool but laying the foundation for a more just and responsible society. The collective effort of the government, technology partners, and citizens will ensure that Bharat takes a significant step towards becoming a nation where accountability and transparency are not just ideals but everyday realities. Through this app, every citizen can play a role in building a better, safer Bharat, proving that together, we can achieve great things.

CHAPTER TWENTY-EIGHT

THE FARMER SUICIDE CRISIS

As I sit to pen down the challenges that confront our great nation, one issue haunts me deeply—our farmers, the very backbone of Bharat, are taking their own lives. These suicides aren't just individual tragedies; they are a national crisis. The future of India, the dream of transforming our country into Vishwaguru, cannot be realized if those who till our soil, who feed our people, are forced into such hopelessness. To see a farmer, who represents our land's fertility, prosperity, and potential, succumb to despair is a wound on the soul of our nation. The time has come to address this crisis head-on, for in the welfare of our farmers lies the welfare of our country.

The issue of farmer suicides is not just about individual suffering; it reflects deep-rooted systemic problems—crippling debt, unpredictable weather, insufficient support from the government, and ineffective agricultural policies. These problems have compounded over decades, pushing the farmers of Bharat, once proud and self-reliant, into a dark abyss. This is not the vision I have for our great nation. If Bharat is to become a global leader, Vishwaguru, then the welfare of every farmer must be paramount. We cannot let them fall; their prosperity is intricately linked to the prosperity of our nation.

The Problem:

India's agriculture sector has been witnessing a disturbing trend for decades—rising farmer suicides. Between 1995 and 2019, over 300,000 farmers took their own lives due to economic distress, crop failures, and insurmountable debt. This is not merely an economic issue but a social tragedy. The primary reasons for these suicides include crop failures due to erratic monsoons, the heavy burden of loans, and a lack of governmental support during crises.

A poignant story comes from Maharashtra's Vidarbha region, where a farmer took his life after a series of crop failures left him deep in debt. He had taken loans from both the formal banking system and private moneylenders, only to see his crops wither under the drought. Faced with the inability to repay his loans and the looming threat of losing his land, he saw no other escape. His story mirrors those of thousands of other farmers, whose deaths serve as a haunting reminder of the urgent reforms needed in the sector.

Solutions according to Varad Tikam

Debt Relief and Financial Aid

The most pressing problem for farmers is the crushing burden of debt. Many farmers, particularly small and marginal ones, are trapped in a vicious cycle of borrowing money to plant crops, only to see their yields destroyed by drought or unseasonal rain. For many, the loans they take out become impossible to repay, leading to desperation.

The government has introduced loan waivers, but these are temporary and provide only a short-lived respite. A more sustainable solution would be the introduction of a comprehensive **Debt Relief Commission** that focuses on restructuring loans rather than waiving them. Farmers should have access to low-interest loans, especially during crises like droughts or crop failures. The commission would also oversee informal lending, regulating moneylenders who often charge exorbitant rates.

Consider Telangana's innovative **Rythu Bandhu Scheme**, which provides farmers with direct investment support for every cropping season. The scheme offers   ₹5,000 per acre per season, enabling farmers to invest in seeds, fertilizers, and other necessary inputs without resorting to loans. Expanding such programs across the nation could significantly reduce the financial pressure on farmers and prevent indebtedness.

Irrigation Infrastructure and Sustainable Farming Practices

A critical factor behind the distress in the farming sector is India's over-reliance on monsoon rains. Less than half of India's agricultural land is irrigated, leaving millions of farmers vulnerable to droughts and erratic rainfall. In regions like Vidarbha and Marathwada in Maharashtra, repeated droughts have led to massive crop failures and farmer suicides.

We need to invest in irrigation infrastructure on a war footing. Large-scale projects like the **Pradhan Mantri Krishi Sinchai Yojana** (PMKSY), aimed at improving irrigation access, must be expanded. The scheme seeks to expand irrigation coverage and promote efficient water use by introducing drip and sprinkler irrigation systems. However, its reach must be increased to cover more regions and crops. The government should also incentivize rainwater harvesting and micro-irrigation techniques at the village level, making water available year-round for farmers.

The **Telangana Mission Kakatiya** project serves as a model in this regard. The government restored more than 45,000 irrigation tanks across the state, providing a reliable water source for farmers even during times of drought. This has led to a sharp increase in agricultural productivity and reduced dependence on monsoons.

Crop Diversification and Organic Farming

Monoculture—the practice of growing only one type of crop—has rendered farmers more vulnerable to crop failures and market fluctuations. For instance, in states like Punjab and Haryana, farmers primarily grow wheat and rice, both of which are heavily dependent on water. When these crops fail, farmers have no other sources of income.

The government must promote **crop diversification**, encouraging farmers to grow a mix of crops that are more resilient to climatic changes and require less water. Additionally, the switch to **organic farming** should be incentivized. Organic farming is not only environmentally sustainable but also reduces the dependency on chemical fertilizers and pesticides, which are often expensive and contribute to farmer debt.

In Sikkim, where organic farming has been adopted on a wide scale, farmers are reaping the benefits of higher profits and lower input costs. Sikkim became the first fully organic state in India, showing that with the right policies, sustainable farming is possible without sacrificing productivity.

Market Access and Fair Pricing

A significant issue that pushes farmers into distress is the lack of access to fair markets and prices for their produce. Even when farmers manage to grow a good crop, they are often exploited by middlemen and forced to sell their produce at low prices. The **Minimum Support Price (MSP)** system, while helpful, is not uniformly implemented across all states or crops, leaving farmers at the mercy of market fluctuations.

To ensure that farmers receive fair prices for their produce, the **e-NAM (National Agriculture Market)** platform must be strengthened. e-NAM connects farmers directly with buyers across India, allowing them to sell their produce without the interference of middlemen. Expanding the platform to include more farmers, crops, and states will empower farmers with better market access and price discovery.

Social and Psychological Support

While financial assistance and market reforms are crucial, the psychological toll of farming cannot be ignored. The shame and social stigma associated with debt and failure often drive farmers to despair. There is a need for a comprehensive mental health support system for farmers, where counseling and support are available in rural areas. The **Kisan Call Centers**, which currently offer technical advice to farmers, could be expanded to include mental health services.

Real-life stories illustrate the importance of this support. In Andhra Pradesh, the wife of a farmer who committed suicide shared that her husband had become increasingly withdrawn and depressed before taking his life. If there had been more avenues for psychological support, perhaps his life could have been saved.

Conclusion:

As I bring this chapter to a close, I am reminded of the immense responsibility we have as a nation. Our farmers are the heart of Bharat, and their well-being is critical to our country's future. The solutions I've outlined—financial aid, irrigation reform, crop diversification, market access, and social support—are not just policy recommendations but a call to action. If implemented with the seriousness they deserve, they will help us rescue our farmers from despair and rebuild their confidence.

A prosperous Bharat cannot exist without prosperous farmers. As we march toward becoming Vishwaguru, we must ensure that those who nourish our land and feed our people are no longer pushed to the brink. Together, we can create a future where no farmer feels so desperate that death is their only escape. It is time we give back to the hands that have fed us for generations.s

CHAPTER TWENTY-NINE

OUTDATED DEFENSE EQUIPMENT

As I contemplate India's defense sector, one issue stands out with increasing urgency: our dependence on outdated equipment. This is more than a mere technical challenge; it's a significant concern for our national security and our aspiration to be recognized as a global power. Modernizing our military capabilities is not just about keeping pace with technological advancements; it's about ensuring that we are prepared for the evolving threats of the 21st century. As we strive to position India as Vishwaguru, addressing this issue is paramount. The need to upgrade our defense equipment aligns directly with our vision of a secure, self-reliant, and influential India on the global stage. Let us delve into the problems associated with outdated defense equipment, and explore real-life incidents that highlight these issues, and I have comprehensive solutions to address them.

The Problems

Technological Obsolescence:

The issue of technological obsolescence is glaring in several instances. Take the example of the Indian Air Force's (IAF) MiG-21 fighter jets. These aircraft, which were introduced in the 1960s, have been the backbone of our air fleet for decades. However, their outdated technology poses significant risks. On January 21, 2021, a MiG-21 crashed during a training flight near Gwalior, tragically resulting in the death of the pilot. The incident was a stark reminder of the perils associated with maintaining an aging fleet. According to a Times of India report, over 200 MiG-21 aircraft were involved in accidents between 1970 and 2020, reflecting serious safety and reliability concerns [Source: Times of India, 2021].

Another example is the state of our naval fleet. The INS Vikramaditya, a refurbished aircraft carrier, was commissioned into the Indian Navy in 2013. Despite its strategic importance, it has faced numerous issues, including frequent breakdowns and maintenance challenges. These problems underscore the need for more modern and reliable naval assets to ensure effective maritime security [Source: The Hindu, 2022].

Maintenance and Reliability Issues:

Maintenance issues are another significant challenge. During the 2016 surgical strikes across the Line of Control (LoC), the Indian Army's reliance on older artillery systems, such as the 130mm Bofors guns, became evident. The Bofors guns, which were purchased in the 1980s, have experienced considerable wear and tear. The Hindu Business Line reported that these older systems have struggled with maintenance issues, impacting their operational reliability [Source: Hindu Business Line, 2017]. The maintenance challenges associated with older equipment not only strain our defense budget but also affect the readiness of our forces.

The 2016 surgical strikes highlighted how outdated artillery systems can hinder operational effectiveness. The limited range and precision of older artillery compared to newer systems used by adversaries can impact the effectiveness of such strategic operations.

Training Gaps:

Training gaps resulting from outdated equipment were glaringly evident during the 2020 Galwan Valley clash with China. During this skirmish, Indian soldiers faced significant challenges due to inadequate and outdated gear. The clash exposed deficiencies in our cold-weather gear and surveillance equipment, which were not up to par compared to the advanced technology possessed by the Chinese forces. The Economic Times reported that our soldiers were ill-equipped compared to their counterparts, who had superior technology and training [Source: Economic Times, 2020]. This training gap underscores the need for continuous updates and modernization in our defense training programs to align with the latest technological advancements.

Furthermore, outdated equipment impacts the ability of our forces to adapt to new combat scenarios. For instance, the lack of advanced night-vision equipment and modern communication systems can hinder our troops' effectiveness in low-visibility situations and complex operational environments.

Strategic Disadvantage:

The strategic vulnerabilities of outdated equipment were evident during the 2019 Balakot airstrike. While the operation demonstrated the capabilities of the Indian Air Force, it also revealed limitations in some older systems. The lack of advanced electronic warfare systems and modern avionics in certain aircraft affected their effectiveness. According to an analysis by the International Institute for Strategic Studies, outdated technology limited the precision and efficiency of the strike [Source: International Institute for Strategic Studies, 2019]. The strategic disadvantage posed by outdated equipment highlights the necessity for continual upgrades to maintain a competitive edge in global defense scenarios.

Additionally, outdated defense systems can create vulnerabilities in areas such as cyber warfare. As adversaries enhance their cyber capabilities, having robust and modern systems is crucial for defending against sophisticated cyber-attacks.

Solutions according to Varad Tikam

Comprehensive Modernization Plan:

A strategic modernization plan should be developed to address both immediate and long-term needs. This plan should include a thorough evaluation of our current capabilities, identification of critical gaps, and investment in cutting-edge technology. For example, the Indian Navy's proposal to replace older submarines with advanced Scorpène-class submarines represents a step in the right direction [Source: The Hindu, 2020]. However, this effort should be expanded to cover all branches of the military, including air defense, artillery, and communications.

The modernization plan should prioritize upgrading critical systems such as air defense missiles, naval vessels, and radar systems. Investments in advanced technologies like hypersonic missiles and next-generation fighter jets should be considered to enhance our strategic capabilities.

Enhanced Research and Development (R&D):

Investing in R&D is crucial for developing next-generation defense technologies. Collaboration between the government, private sector, and academic institutions can drive innovation and accelerate the development of advanced systems. For instance, the DRDO's development of the Akash missile system demonstrates the potential of indigenous R&D [Source: Defense Research and Development Organisation, 2021]. Expanding such initiatives can help us reduce dependency on foreign technology and build a more self-reliant defense sector.

R&D efforts should focus on emerging technologies such as artificial intelligence, advanced drone systems, and quantum encryption. By fostering innovation and supporting domestic defense startups, we can create a robust ecosystem for technological advancements.

Revamping the Procurement Process:

Streamlining the procurement process is essential for reducing delays and inefficiencies. The bureaucratic hurdles and lengthy approval processes in acquiring new defense equipment have been a persistent issue. Establishing a dedicated defense procurement agency with greater autonomy and efficiency could address these challenges. This agency should oversee acquisitions, ensure transparency, and implement best practices in procurement [Source: Ministry of Defense, India, 2022].

The procurement process should include mechanisms for rapid acquisition of critical systems and emergency procurement procedures to address urgent needs. Additionally, fostering partnerships with private defense firms and international suppliers can facilitate timely acquisitions and technology transfers.

Building Strategic Alliances:

Forming strategic alliances with other nations can enhance our defense capabilities and provide access to advanced technologies. Collaborations with countries that are leaders in defense technology, such as the United States and Israel, can offer opportunities for technology transfer and joint development projects. For instance, the Indo-US defense cooperation agreements have facilitated the acquisition of advanced systems like Apache helicopters [Source: US Department of Defense, 2019]. Expanding such alliances can help us gain access to cutting-edge equipment and enhance our defense capabilities.

Additionally, participating in multinational defense exercises and joint training programs can help our forces adapt to new technologies and combat scenarios. Building strong defense partnerships can also provide strategic leverage in geopolitical negotiations.

Improving Training and Simulation Facilities:

Upgrading training and simulation facilities is essential for preparing our personnel to operate modern equipment. Investing in state-of-the-art simulators and realistic training environments can bridge the gap between current capabilities and future needs. The Indian Army's adoption of the Simulation-Based Training System is a positive development, but broader implementation is needed across all branches [Source: Indian Army, 2021].

Training programs should incorporate advanced simulation technologies to provide realistic scenarios for combat, maintenance, and operational procedures. Enhancing training facilities and incorporating modern equipment in training exercises will ensure that our personnel are proficient in using the latest defense technologies.

Legislative and Policy Reforms:

Institutionalizing the modernization process through legislative and policy reforms can provide a structured framework for defense upgrades. The proposed Defense Modernization Act should include provisions for streamlined procurement, increased funding for domestic production, and enhanced oversight. This legislative framework will ensure that modernization efforts are consistent with national security objectives and that resources are allocated efficiently.

The act should also establish clear guidelines for technology acquisition, domestic production incentives, and R&D investments. Creating a Defense Modernization Committee to oversee the implementation of the act will help ensure transparency and accountability in defense modernization efforts.

Conclusion:

The challenges posed by outdated defense equipment are multifaceted, impacting our operational effectiveness, strategic posture, and national security. As we confront these challenges, it is clear that modernization is not just a necessity but a strategic imperative. Our commitment to addressing these issues through a comprehensive and strategic approach will enhance our national security and bolster our global standing. By embracing the proposed solutions and reforms, we can ensure that India's defense sector is well-equipped to meet the demands of the 21st century.

The path forward requires a collective effort, combining technological innovation, strategic partnerships, and legislative support. Let us move forward with determination and foresight, understanding that our efforts today will shape the security and prosperity of India for generations to come. Our responsibility is to act decisively and strategically, ensuring that India stands resilient and powerful on the global stage, ready to face the challenges of the future.

CHAPTER THIRTY

LACK OF RESEARCH AND DEVELOPMENT (R&D) INVESTMENT

When we speak about the future of Bharat, the question that arises is, "What will make India a global leader in technology and innovation?" The answer lies in one crucial area that has been long neglected—Research and Development (R&D). As we envision India as Vishwaguru, it is imperative to ask ourselves whether we are truly investing in the future. The answer, unfortunately, is disheartening. India spends a mere 0.7% of its GDP on R&D, lagging far behind nations like the United States, which allocates over 3%, or South Korea, where R&D spending exceeds 4% of GDP. If we don't act now, we will struggle to secure our place as a technological leader.

This chapter is not merely a critique but a call to action. Our country stands at a critical juncture where the decisions we make today will determine whether we continue to be a nation of followers or rise to become a leader in global innovation. I believe that addressing the lack of investment in R&D is not just a matter of national development but a responsibility we owe to future generations. It is time we act, and act decisively, to ensure that our children inherit a country capable of leading the world in technological advancements.

The Problem:

India's lack of sufficient investment in R&D is a severe bottleneck in the nation's growth trajectory. According to the Economic Survey of India (2021-22), India's R&D expenditure has stagnated at 0.7% of GDP over the last decade, which is far below the global average of 2.3%. This has far-reaching consequences for technological innovation, economic growth, and national security.

A stark example of this neglect is India's reliance on foreign technology in sectors such as defense and pharmaceuticals. Take the case of India's indigenous vaccine production during the COVID-19 pandemic. While India excelled in manufacturing vaccines, the core technologies for developing mRNA vaccines were sourced from countries like the U.S. and Germany. We should have been a frontrunner in vaccine technology, but our lack of prior investment in R&D made us reliant on external innovation. The gap between where we stand and where we should be is widening with each passing day. Real-life incidents like this expose the urgent need to invest heavily in R&D if we are to reduce our dependency and become self-sufficient.

The problem becomes even more alarming when considering sectors critical to the future, such as artificial intelligence (AI), quantum computing, and biotechnology. While countries like China and the U.S. are investing billions in these fields, India remains far behind. The NITI Aayog's report on AI in 2019 highlighted that India's public and private sectors combined invested just $1 billion in AI, compared to China's $70 billion. Without robust investments, we risk missing out on the fourth industrial revolution.

Solutions according to Varad Tikam

Increasing the R&D Budget to 2% of GDP

To address the issue of inadequate R&D investment, it is essential for India to significantly boost its expenditure in this area. Currently, India allocates only about 0.7% of its GDP to research and development, which is insufficient when compared to global standards. Countries like the United

States and South Korea invest over 3% and 4% of their GDP in R&D, respectively. To bridge this gap, India should aim to increase its R&D budget to 2% of GDP in the short term, with a long-term goal of reaching 4% by 2030.

Achieving this increase requires a strategic reallocation of national resources. The government should consider diverting funds from less critical areas and focusing them on R&D activities. This reallocation can be complemented by encouraging private-sector investment. Offering tax incentives and grants to companies that invest in research will create a favorable environment for private contributions to R&D. Additionally, establishing a dedicated R&D fund managed by a central body, such as the proposed National R&D Council, will ensure that resources are efficiently allocated to various research projects and institutions.

However, this strategy is not without challenges. One major obstacle is the financial constraint of increasing R&D expenditure. To overcome this, the government can explore alternative funding mechanisms, such as public-private partnerships and international collaborations. Ensuring that the increased budget is effectively utilized requires administrative efficiency. The proposed National R&D Council can oversee and streamline fund allocation, ensuring transparency and accountability in the utilization of resources.

Establishing a National R&D Council

The creation of a National R&D Council (NRDC) will play a pivotal role in centralizing the oversight and coordination of research and development activities. This council would serve as a strategic body responsible for setting R&D priorities, allocating funds, and fostering collaboration between various stakeholders, including government ministries, universities, research institutions, and the private sector.

The NRDC should be composed of experts from diverse fields, including science, technology, and industry, as well as representatives from government agencies. This diverse composition will ensure that the council can address various aspects of R&D and align its efforts with national priorities. The NRDC's responsibilities would include defining national research agendas, managing research grants, and monitoring the progress of funded projects. Additionally, establishing innovation hubs within key research institutions and universities will further enhance the effectiveness of the NRDC's initiatives.

Despite the potential benefits, the establishment of the NRDC may face bureaucratic challenges. To mitigate this, the council should be granted clear mandates and operational authority while coordinating with existing agencies. Ensuring effective coordination between the NRDC and other stakeholders is crucial. Regular meetings and progress reports can help maintain alignment and address any issues that arise.

Reforming Educational Institutions and Promoting Innovation

Fostering a culture of innovation within India's educational institutions is essential for long-term success in R&D. Reforming the education system to prioritize research and innovation will ensure that the next generation of researchers and technologists is well-prepared to contribute to India's growth in these areas.

Increased funding for research programs at universities and research institutes is a fundamental step. This includes providing grants for innovative projects, supporting doctoral and post-doctoral research, and investing in state-of-the-art research facilities. Revising curricula to emphasize research and innovation will encourage students to engage in research activities and pursue careers in this field. Offering training programs for faculty members to keep them updated with the latest research methodologies and technologies is also crucial.

Additionally, creating incubation centers within universities to support student-led startups and entrepreneurial ventures will foster an environment of innovation. These centers should provide mentorship, funding, and resources to help students turn their research ideas into viable products and services.

Challenges such as resistance to change and resource allocation may arise during the implementation of these reforms. Engaging stakeholders, including educators, students, and industry experts, in the reform process can help address resistance and demonstrate the long-term benefits of the changes. Ensuring equitable distribution of resources across institutions requires establishing criteria for funding allocation based on performance and alignment with national priorities.

Conclusion:

As I conclude this chapter, I urge my fellow Indians to realize that the future of our nation rests on the foundation of knowledge, innovation, and scientific advancement. The lack of investment in R&D is not just a gap in our economic policy; it is a gap in our vision for Bharat. If we do not act now, we will continue to depend on others for technology and solutions that we should be developing ourselves.

This is not merely a financial issue—it is a matter of national pride, a responsibility to our ancestors, and an obligation to our future. Increasing R&D investment, creating a National R&D Council, and fostering innovation in our educational institutions will transform Bharat into the Vishwaguru we aspire to be. Let us not delay this any further. The time for action is now, and it is my firm belief that by addressing this critical issue, we are one step closer to making India a global leader.

India's path to becoming a global leader in technology and innovation is fraught with challenges, but through collective will, increased investment, and a commitment to fostering research, we can overcome them. As the Bhagavad Gita teaches, action is our responsibility. The rest will follow.

CHAPTER THIRTY-ONE

OVERREGULATION AND RED TAPE IN INDIA

As I stand at the cusp of envisioning a future where India emerges as a global leader, I find myself grappling with a question that haunts the minds of many reformists: why, despite having immense potential, does our nation falter in the global ease of doing business rankings? The answer is as clear as it is disheartening—our regulatory framework, bogged down by overregulation and red tape, is choking the entrepreneurial spirit of our people. These outdated and complex regulations stifle innovation and make it incredibly difficult for domestic and foreign investors to navigate the Indian market.

If we are to make India the Vishwaguru—the guiding light of the world—this is one of the first, most pressing issues that we must tackle head-on. The process of doing business in India must be seamless, efficient, and welcoming to innovation. It's not merely about encouraging foreign investment; it's about unleashing the full potential of our own people. Every Indian entrepreneur, startup, and business entity must be able to flourish without unnecessary governmental roadblocks. The path to greatness begins with ensuring that our systems foster growth rather than impede it.

The Problem: Overregulation and Red Tape

India's regulatory framework has long been characterized by excessive bureaucracy, archaic laws, and overlapping regulations. According to the World Bank's 2020 "Ease of Doing Business" report, India ranked 63rd globally, an improvement but still far from ideal for a nation aspiring to be a global leader. However, the crux of the problem lies deeper in the inefficiency of India's bureaucratic machinery. The multiple layers of permissions, licenses, and compliance requirements often result in unnecessary delays, discouraging both domestic and foreign businesses from investing in the country.

Take, for example, the case of IKEA, which first showed interest in the Indian market as early as 2009. It took the company several years of navigating complex regulations before it could open its first store in 2018. IKEA faced numerous hurdles, including issues related to India's Foreign Direct Investment (FDI) policies, sourcing requirements, and local labor laws. Such stories are not isolated; rather, they reflect the systemic nature of the problem. Businesses often face regulatory hurdles that are not only time-consuming but also expensive, making it easier to set up operations in countries like China or Vietnam, where the regulatory environment is more streamlined.

The issue of overregulation also affects Indian entrepreneurs, particularly those in the Small and Medium Enterprises (SME) sector. A report by the Centre for Civil Society highlighted that a small business in India requires nearly 25 licenses and registrations to operate legally. Such cumbersome processes not only stifle the growth of small businesses but also encourage corruption, as companies often resort to bribes to expedite processes.

Real-Life Example: Tata Nano Project

One of the most striking examples of how red tape can derail even the most ambitious projects is the Tata Nano project. Tata Motors had envisioned the Nano as the world's cheapest car, a revolutionary product for the Indian market. However, the project was plagued by regulatory hurdles from the beginning. The company initially chose Singur in West Bengal as the manufacturing site, but land acquisition issues and bureaucratic delays led to significant protests, forcing Tata Motors to shift the project to Gujarat. The project's delays and complications contributed to the Nano's ultimate commercial failure. This case illustrates how regulatory inefficiency can stifle innovation and delay progress, even for established corporations.

Solutions according to Varad Tikam

The Promise of a Single Window Clearance System (SWCS)

Picture this: A Single Window Clearance System (SWCS) that consolidates all regulatory approvals under one digital roof. Instead of grappling with multiple departments, businesses could submit their documents once and receive all necessary clearances within a set timeframe. This system would not only bring transparency but also eliminate redundant steps, reducing delays and inefficiencies.

However, the road to implementing SWCS is fraught with challenges. Coordination among various government departments, each with its own set of regulations and procedures, is no small feat. Achieving seamless integration will require more than just technological advancements; it demands political will, policy alignment, and significant investment in technology.

To address these challenges, the central government could mandate all departments to integrate their services with the SWCS platform. Robust software systems would be crucial for streamlining communication between departments. Legislative backing, coupled with training and sensitization programs for government officials, would ensure that the system operates smoothly and efficiently.

The Digital Revolution

Moving beyond the SWCS, envision a future where the Indian bureaucracy sheds its reliance on outdated paperwork and manual processes. The digitization of regulatory procedures—such as filing for permits, tax compliance, and business registrations—holds the promise of a faster, more transparent system. The "Digital India" program has laid the groundwork, but there is still much work to be done, especially in rural and less developed areas.

The shift to a fully digital environment means businesses could manage their regulatory needs entirely online, without the need to physically visit government offices. Yet, this transition faces obstacles, including outdated infrastructure, limited digital literacy among officials, and cybersecurity concerns.

To overcome these hurdles, the government must invest in upgrading digital infrastructure, provide comprehensive training for officials, and ensure robust data security measures. A phased approach—starting with urban centers and gradually extending to rural areas—could make the transition smoother. Implementing blockchain technology could further enhance data security and transparency, making tampering with records nearly impossible.

Streamlining Regulations

The sheer complexity of India's regulatory framework—marked by outdated laws and overlapping regulations—often overwhelms businesses, particularly small and medium enterprises. Many laws, remnants of colonial rule, are no longer relevant in today's context. Simplifying and rationalizing these regulations is crucial.

A Regulatory Reform Commission could spearhead this effort, reviewing outdated laws and consolidating conflicting regulations. Sector-specific frameworks would make it easier for businesses to navigate the system by focusing on industry-specific needs. This overhaul would not only streamline compliance but also ensure that regulations remain relevant and effective.

Addressing Sector-Specific Challenges

Different sectors face unique regulatory challenges. For example, the manufacturing industry deals with complex environmental regulations, while the tech sector struggles with outdated intellectual property laws. Tailoring reforms to address these specific issues would foster innovation and growth.

By engaging with industry stakeholders and implementing pilot programs, the government can test these reforms and make necessary adjustments before a national rollout. This targeted approach ensures that reforms meet sector-specific needs while maintaining essential protections.

Fighting Corruption Through Transparency

Corruption remains a persistent issue within India's regulatory system. Businesses often resort to bribery to expedite approvals due to the opaque nature of the current system. Increasing transparency and accountability is essential to combat corruption.

Technology can play a significant role here, with digitized processes and blockchain tracking ensuring that every step in the approval process is visible and auditable. Strengthening anti-corruption laws and establishing independent watchdogs to monitor compliance and investigate complaints are also crucial measures.

A Vision for a New Era

As we look towards the future, the need for regulatory reform in India is evident. The goal is to create an environment where businesses can thrive without being bogged down by bureaucratic obstacles. The vision is to transform India into a global leader in innovation and economic growth—an aspiration that requires a regulatory framework that is efficient, transparent, and supportive of entrepreneurship.

This vision demands bold action and sustained effort. By implementing the Single Window Clearance System, digitizing regulatory processes, simplifying regulations, and tackling corruption, we can unlock India's vast potential. The time for this transformation is now. If we want to lead the world, we must first liberate our potential from the shackles of red tape.

Conclusion

In conclusion, the solutions to overregulation and red tape in India are clear but require bold and sustained action. From implementing a Single Window Clearance System to digitizing regulatory processes, simplifying regulations, and tackling corruption, each step will bring us closer to an environment where businesses can flourish. These reforms are not just technical changes—they are transformative initiatives that can unlock India's vast potential.

The goal is clear: to make India the Vishwaguru, a global leader in innovation, entrepreneurship, and economic growth. This vision demands a regulatory framework that is efficient, transparent, and conducive to business, one that empowers every Indian entrepreneur to succeed without being weighed down by bureaucratic hurdles. The time for action is now. If we want to truly lead the world, we must first liberate our potential from the shackles of red tape.

CHAPTER THIRTY-TWO

वतिरक (VITARAK)

In the digital age, the presence of a robust, secure, and cost-effective web hosting service is crucial for the growth and sustainability of businesses, government agencies, and individuals. As India advances toward a more digitally integrated society, the need for a dependable and accessible web hosting solution becomes increasingly significant. To address this pressing need, I propose the creation of a revolutionary company named Vitarak. This state-sponsored enterprise aims to transform the web hosting landscape in India by offering a suite of benefits, including free *.ind* domain registration, unparalleled security, market-leading affordability, and cutting-edge performance. Vitarak will also play a pivotal role in hosting government websites, with a distinctive approach to server management to ensure the utmost security and reliability.

Concept of Vitarak

Vitarak will be a government-backed enterprise dedicated to providing high-quality web hosting services across India. Its core mission is to democratize web hosting by offering it at the lowest cost possible while maintaining high standards of security, speed, and reliability. The term "Vitarak," meaning "distributor" in Hindi, embodies the company's goal of distributing advanced digital resources to all sectors of Indian society, from individual entrepreneurs to large government agencies.

Core Features and Benefits

Free .ind Domain Registration

One of Vitarak's standout features is the provision of free .ind domain registrations. This initiative will enable Indian businesses, government agencies, and individuals to secure a unique and nationally significant online identity. By using the .ind domain, users will not only establish a local digital presence but also contribute to the enhancement of India's digital sovereignty.

Affordable Hosting Solutions

Vitarak will offer the most competitive rates in the market, providing top-tier web hosting solutions at unprecedentedly low costs. By leveraging government support and cutting-edge technology, Vitarak will make high-quality hosting accessible to startups, SMEs, and individual entrepreneurs. This affordability will help stimulate innovation and economic growth across various sectors.

Unmatched Security

Security is a top priority for Vitarak. The company will implement a multi-layered security approach, including advanced firewalls, intrusion detection systems, and regular security updates. Vitarak will also adopt best practices in data encryption and threat management to protect user data from cyber threats. This commitment to security will be critical for maintaining user trust and safeguarding sensitive information.

High Performance and Reliability

Vitarak will prioritize performance by investing in the latest server technology and infrastructure. High-speed SSD storage, load balancing, and global content delivery networks (CDNs) will ensure fast website load times and minimal downtime. By maintaining a focus on performance, Vitarak will provide a seamless and efficient user experience.

Dedicated Government Hosting

Vitarak will play a pivotal role in hosting government websites, ensuring that critical public services and information remain secure and accessible. Special protocols will be established to manage these sites, including rigorous security measures and regular audits. To further protect sensitive information, government servers will be physically and logically isolated from each other, preventing potential cross-contamination and reducing the risk of widespread disruptions.

Server Management and Isolation

A distinctive feature of Vitarak's infrastructure will be its approach to server management. Servers will be designed to be isolated from each other, both physically and virtually. This strategy involves placing servers in separate data centers and implementing network segmentation to prevent unauthorized access and mitigate risks associated with potential breaches. The isolated architecture will enhance overall security and ensure that each server operates independently, reducing the impact of any single point of failure.

Scalable Solutions

Vitarak will offer scalable hosting solutions to accommodate the varying needs of its users. From small personal websites to large enterprise applications, Vitarak will provide flexible hosting plans that can be easily scaled up or down based on user requirements. This scalability will ensure that users can grow their digital presence without the need for constant migration or service disruptions.

Environmental Responsibility

In alignment with global sustainability trends, Vitarak will adopt environmentally friendly practices in its operations. The company will invest in energy-efficient data centers, utilize renewable energy sources where possible, and implement strategies to minimize its carbon footprint. By focusing on sustainability, Vitarak will contribute to India's green initiatives and promote responsible digital infrastructure.

User-Friendly Interface and Support

Vitarak will offer an intuitive and user-friendly interface for managing web hosting services. The platform will include a comprehensive control panel, easy-to-use website builders, and detailed analytics to help users optimize their websites. Additionally, a dedicated customer support team will be available 24/7 to assist with technical issues, provide guidance, and ensure a smooth user experience.

Community and Educational Initiatives

Vitarak will also engage in community outreach and educational initiatives to promote digital literacy and web development skills. Workshops, webinars, and online resources will be provided to help users understand the benefits of web hosting, learn about best practices, and build effective online presences. These initiatives will foster a culture of digital innovation and empowerment across India.

Implementation Strategy

To bring Vitarak to fruition, a detailed implementation strategy will be necessary:

Government Partnership and Funding

The establishment of Vitarak will require strong government support and funding. The government will provide initial capital, regulatory backing, and strategic oversight. Public-private partnerships will be explored to secure additional resources and expertise.

Infrastructure Development

Vitarak will invest in state-of-the-art data centers and server technology. Partnerships with leading technology providers will ensure access to the latest hardware and software. Data centers will be strategically located to provide optimal performance and redundancy.

Security Protocols and Compliance

The company will implement robust security protocols and adhere to national and international data protection standards. Regular security assessments and audits will be conducted to maintain high levels of security.

Market Outreach and User Education

A comprehensive marketing campaign will be launched to promote Vitarak's services. The company will also provide educational resources to help users understand the benefits of its offerings and make the most of its features.

Customer Support and Service Excellence

Vitarak will establish a dedicated customer support team to assist users with technical issues and inquiries. A focus on service excellence will ensure that users receive timely and effective support.

Conclusion

Vitarak represents a groundbreaking initiative to enhance India's digital infrastructure. By offering free .ind domains, affordable hosting solutions, and unparalleled security and performance, Vitarak will empower businesses, government agencies, and individuals across the nation. Its innovative approach to server management, commitment to environmental responsibility, and focus on community engagement will set a new standard for web hosting in India. As India continues its digital transformation, Vitarak will be at the forefront, driving progress and ensuring that the nation's digital future is secure, accessible, and prosperous.

CHAPTER THIRTY-THREE

THE BRAIN DRAIN PHENOMENON

As I sit to reflect on the journey of our great nation, the question that constantly comes to mind is this: how do we transform Bharat into Vishwaguru—a global leader in innovation, economy, and culture? One of the biggest hurdles we face in this mission is the *brain drain phenomenon.* Many of our brightest minds, equipped with world-class education, innovation, and expertise, are leaving the shores of India for opportunities abroad. This isn't merely a loss of human capital; it's a blow to the potential India holds to reshape its future and the future of the world.

The urgency to address brain drain cannot be overstated. Every year, thousands of engineers, doctors, scientists, and entrepreneurs leave our country. If we are to build a nation that competes globally, we need to retain this talent. By doing so, we will not only prevent the intellectual exodus but also strengthen India's foundation for becoming Vishwaguru. The issue of brain drain, in my view, is a reflection of deeper systemic problems—problems that we can and must resolve if we are to reclaim our place as a global leader.

The Problem of Brain Drain

The phenomenon of brain drain is not new to India. It dates back to the post-independence era when many students sought higher education abroad and chose to stay there. In recent decades, however, the magnitude has increased. A 2020 study by the Ministry of External Affairs found that over **17.5 million Indians were living abroad**, many of whom are highly skilled professionals. In sectors like IT, healthcare, and engineering, Indian experts lead major multinational companies, hospitals, and tech enterprises abroad. For instance, CEOs like Satya Nadella of Microsoft and Sundar Pichai of Google are perfect examples of Indian talent contributing to foreign economies.

The reasons for this exodus are manifold—better job opportunities, higher salaries, advanced research facilities, and overall superior quality of life in developed nations. Take the case of Dr. Venkatraman Ramakrishnan, who won the Nobel Prize in Chemistry in 2009. Despite being educated in India, he spent the majority of his career working in the United States and the United Kingdom. His contributions to science are commendable, but imagine if such minds were working within our own borders, pushing the frontiers of Indian science.

The loss of this talent comes at a significant cost. It weakens India's competitive edge in global research and innovation, creates a vacuum of skilled professionals, and results in missed opportunities for economic growth. According to a report by the Organisation for Economic Co-operation and Development (OECD), over **30% of Indian-born professionals working abroad** have advanced degrees, highlighting the caliber of the human capital we are losing. India, instead of being a hub for innovation, has become a talent exporter.

Systemic Issues

The root cause of brain drain lies in the systemic issues that plague our country—lack of research funding, outdated infrastructure, and an education system that prioritizes rote learning over creativity. Even our industries often fail to offer competitive salaries and the intellectual freedom that global organizations provide.

For example, in 2018, a 23-year-old IIT graduate left for Silicon Valley after working for a year in Bengaluru. His reason was simple—while the pay abroad was higher, the intellectual freedom and access to cutting-edge technology were incomparable to what Indian companies offered. Such examples underscore the need for radical reforms if we are to retain talent.

Solutions According to Varad Tikam

Investing in Research and Development (R&D)

Imagine a young scientist, Priya, who has just completed her PhD in a cutting-edge field like quantum computing from an esteemed Indian university. Her research has the potential to revolutionize technology, but the facilities and funding available in India are limited. She receives an offer from a prestigious research institute in the United States, where the resources are abundant, the infrastructure is state-of-the-art, and the salary package is significantly higher. Unable to resist the lure of these superior opportunities, Priya decides to move abroad, leaving behind a potential breakthrough that could have greatly benefited her home country.

To prevent such scenarios, India must make substantial investments in research and development. Currently, India allocates only around 0.7% of its GDP to R&D, compared to 2-3% in developed countries. To address this gap, I propose the establishment of a National Research and Innovation Fund. This fund would be designed to channel a dedicated percentage of GDP into advancing scientific research and technological development. The allocation would cover state-of-the-art research facilities, competitive salaries for researchers, and grants for innovative projects.

For instance, if this fund were to support initiatives similar to the Atal Innovation Mission, which aims to foster a culture of innovation and entrepreneurship, it could transform the landscape of research in India. With better funding, facilities, and support, researchers like Priya would find it more compelling to remain in India and contribute their talents to national development. However, the challenge here lies in ensuring transparency and accountability in the fund's management. To overcome this, there should be stringent oversight mechanisms, including regular audits and performance reviews, to ensure that funds are used effectively and reach the intended projects.

Creating World-Class Universities and Research Institutes

Consider the story of Rajesh, an aspiring engineer who graduates from one of India's top technical institutes. He dreams of working on advanced robotics and artificial intelligence, but the research infrastructure at his alma mater is outdated. Despite his enthusiasm, the lack of modern tools and collaborative opportunities with international experts leaves him feeling unfulfilled. Rajesh decides to join a leading tech company in Germany, where he has access to cutting-edge technologies and an inspiring work environment.

To prevent this loss of talent, India must focus on creating world-class universities and research institutes. This involves revamping our educational institutions with modern infrastructure, high-tech laboratories, and robust research programs. By establishing Centres of Excellence in various fields such as artificial intelligence, biotechnology, and nanotechnology, India can offer the resources and environment necessary for innovative work.

An example of success in this domain is the Indian Institute of Science (IISc) in Bengaluru, which has made significant strides in research despite facing challenges. Similar models should be replicated across the country, with each Centre of Excellence acting as a hub for advanced research and innovation. However, setting up these centers requires substantial investment and long-term planning. The government should work in collaboration with private sector partners and international organizations to build these centres, ensuring they meet global standards.

Reforming the Job Market and Salaries

Picture Aisha, a talented software developer who excels in her field. She receives job offers from multiple companies, but the compensation and growth prospects offered by Indian companies are not as attractive as those from Silicon Valley or tech giants in Europe. Faced with the choice between a modest salary in India and a lucrative package abroad, Aisha opts for the latter, leaving behind a gap in the local industry.

To address this, India needs to reform its job market and salary structures. The government should initiate public-private partnerships to develop a salary structure that is competitive on a global scale. This involves revising salary benchmarks, offering performance-based incentives, and creating attractive compensation packages that include stock options and professional growth opportunities.

For example, if Indian tech companies were to implement salary and benefit structures similar to those in leading tech hubs, it could encourage skilled professionals like Aisha to stay and contribute to the Indian economy. To support these reforms, there should be a focus on enhancing industry standards and creating a more dynamic job market that aligns with global trends.

Conclusion

The brain drain phenomenon poses a significant challenge to India's aspiration of becoming Vishwaguru. If we are to harness the full potential of our brightest minds, we must address the root causes driving their migration. By investing in R&D, creating world-class educational and research institutions, and reforming the job market, we can create an environment where talent flourishes.

The solutions proposed are not just about retaining skilled individuals—they are about building a robust framework that fosters innovation, supports research, and ensures that our brightest minds have the resources and opportunities they need to thrive in India. As we work towards these goals, we are not only addressing brain drain but also laying the foundation for a future where India leads globally in every sphere.

Let us embrace this challenge with determination and foresight. The responsibility lies with us to build an India where talent is nurtured, opportunities are abundant, and our vision of becoming Vishwaguru is realized. Together, we can make this vision a reality.

CHAPTER THIRTY-FOUR

CORPORATE CONTROL OF MEDIA

As we set forth on the path to transform Bharat into a global leader—Vishwaguru—the role of media cannot be overstated. A well-informed populace forms the backbone of any thriving democracy. However, the growing influence of corporate control over Indian media poses a significant threat to our democratic values. The more the media becomes entwined with corporate interests, the more it veers away from its role as a neutral informant of the people, and this puts the very future of our nation at risk.

Today, I address a crucial issue that is integral to ensuring India remains a healthy democracy: corporate control of the media. If we are to achieve the status of Vishwaguru, we must address the deep-seated problem of media bias that misguides and misinforms our citizens. It is time to reclaim the Fourth Estate and ensure that it remains independent, impartial, and accountable to the people it serves.

The Problem

Corporate Interests in Indian Media

The media, often called the fourth pillar of democracy, plays a vital role in shaping public opinion, disseminating information, and holding those in power accountable. However, when the media becomes entangled with corporate interests, its credibility diminishes, and so does its ability to serve the public.

In India, the media landscape is overwhelmingly controlled by a handful of corporate giants, with top news channels and print media owned by conglomerates with diverse business interests. According to a report by Reporters Without Borders, Indian media's ownership pattern is one of the most concentrated in the world. When media outlets are controlled by corporations with vested interests in sectors such as real estate, energy, or pharmaceuticals, the reporting inevitably becomes biased. Corporate owners often pressure newsrooms to align their editorial stance with their financial goals, silencing stories that could harm their profits or governmental affiliations.

Solutions according to Varad Tikam

Media Ownership Laws

One of the most critical steps in reducing corporate control of Indian media is the establishment of stringent media ownership laws. The concentration of media in the hands of a few large corporations poses a significant threat to unbiased journalism. When a single entity owns multiple media platforms—be it television channels, newspapers, or digital platforms—they can control the narrative and restrict the diversity of opinions and coverage available to the public.

Proposed Solution

India must pass legislation that restricts the amount of media any single corporation can own, both nationally and regionally. This law could cap ownership at 10% of all media outlets, ensuring no one entity holds a majority. Additionally, cross-ownership rules should be enforced so that corporations owning television channels cannot simultaneously own print or digital news media.

Real-Life Example: Media Consolidation in the U.S. In the United States, the Federal Communications Commission (FCC) has long implemented rules to limit media ownership. For example, a single company cannot own both a newspaper and a television station in the same market. This creates a broader diversity of viewpoints and prevents single corporations from dominating public discourse. While these regulations have weakened in recent years, they remain an instructive framework for India.

Challenges & Solutions: One challenge could be resistance from powerful media conglomerates, but strong political will and public pressure can overcome this. The government could also incentivize smaller and independent media outlets with grants, tax breaks, or financial support, encouraging a more decentralized and diverse media ecosystem.

Public Broadcasting Services

Currently, public broadcasters like Doordarshan and All India Radio are seen by many as government mouthpieces rather than impartial sources of information. A reformed public broadcasting system, free from government and corporate interference, would provide an unbiased source of information for citizens.

Proposed Solution:
An independent public broadcasting service should be created, managed by a board that includes representatives from civil society, journalists, and legal experts, and not directly appointed by the government. This board should ensure that editorial independence is protected, and programming reflects a broad range of perspectives, not just those aligned with the ruling party.

Real-Life Example: The BBC The British Broadcasting Corporation (BBC) operates under a Royal Charter that guarantees its independence from both corporate and government influence. The BBC is publicly funded through a television license fee, giving it the financial stability to pursue independent journalism without worrying about corporate advertising revenue or political funding.

Challenges & Solutions: There may be concerns over funding and the potential misuse of power by the independent board. To address this, the board's members should be selected through a transparent process involving multiple institutions, ensuring a diverse and accountable leadership structure. Funding could come from a public media tax, similar to the BBC's model, or from a dedicated public fund.

Independent Journalism Funds: Promoting Investigative Journalism

Investigative journalism is a cornerstone of any democratic society, as it holds power to account. However, in today's media landscape, investigative journalism is often stifled due to its high costs and the risks associated with taking on powerful interests. The increasing reliance on corporate advertising has further diminished the financial independence of news outlets, making it difficult for journalists to pursue hard-hitting stories that might displease corporate owners or advertisers.

Proposed Solution:
The government, in partnership with civil society organizations, should create a national fund for independent journalism. Media outlets and individual journalists should be able to apply for grants to cover investigative work, particularly on issues of public importance like corruption, human rights violations, environmental degradation, and political accountability.

Real-Life Example: ProPublica In the United States, ProPublica is an independent, non-profit newsroom that focuses on investigative journalism in the public interest. Funded by donations and foundations, it has produced award-winning reports on topics such as government corruption, climate change, and healthcare. This model could be replicated in India to support independent reporting without reliance on advertising revenue.

Challenges & Solutions: Ensuring the impartial distribution of funds is key to the success of such a program. The fund should be managed by an autonomous body, comprised of media professionals and public representatives, ensuring that the grants are given based on the merit of proposed investigations rather than political or corporate preferences.

Fact-Checking and Transparency Mechanisms: Ensuring Accountability

In an age of rampant misinformation, particularly through digital platforms, fact-checking has become essential to the survival of democracy. The rise of fake news—often pushed by vested interests—can distort public perception, influence elections, and even incite violence. Unfortunately, corporate media often fails to perform adequate fact-checking due to pressures of speed and financial gain.

Proposed Solution:
India should establish a government-supported but independent fact-checking body tasked with verifying the accuracy of news reports, especially on sensitive political, social, or economic issues. Media outlets should be required by law to submit corrections if found guilty of disseminating false information. Moreover, all media outlets should be mandated to publish transparency reports, detailing their ownership structure, sources of revenue, and any potential conflicts of interest that may affect editorial decisions.

Real-Life Example: Boom and Alt News India already has several fact-checking organizations like Boom and Alt News that work independently to verify and debunk misinformation spread across media platforms. These organizations are good examples of how fact-checking can operate effectively, though they often face legal challenges and threats. By formalizing and supporting such institutions at the national level, India can create a more robust fact-checking ecosystem.

Challenges & Solutions: There could be resistance from media organizations, which might see such regulations as an infringement on their editorial freedom. To mitigate this, transparency mechanisms should be framed as public accountability measures rather than restrictive laws. The fact-checking body must also be carefully insulated from government influence to prevent misuse for political gain.

Encouraging Media Literacy

Finally, media reform isn't only about laws and regulations—it's also about empowering citizens to critically analyze the news they consume. Media literacy, or the ability to evaluate information for its accuracy and bias, is a skill that needs to be promoted through education and public awareness campaigns.

Proposed Solution:
India's education system should integrate media literacy programs at both

school and university levels. These programs would teach students how to identify biased reporting, distinguish between credible and non-credible sources, and understand the influence of corporate ownership on media narratives. Additionally, government-backed public service campaigns could educate the broader population on the importance of critical thinking when consuming news.

Real-Life Example: Finland's Media Literacy Programs Finland is considered one of the world leaders in media literacy. Starting at a young age, Finnish students are taught how to critically assess news and recognize misinformation. As a result, Finland consistently ranks high on global media literacy indexes and experiences lower levels of misinformation compared to other countries.

Challenges & Solutions: Implementing media literacy programs at a national scale requires significant investment in curriculum development and teacher training. However, the long-term benefits—an informed, critically thinking populace—far outweigh the costs. Civil society organizations could also play a key role in developing and promoting these programs in partnership with the government.

Conclusion

In conclusion, corporate control of the media is a serious threat to India's democratic framework. If left unchecked, it will continue to undermine public trust in journalism and misinform the very citizens who form the foundation of our democracy. However, with bold reforms like stringent ownership laws, independent public broadcasting services, a journalism fund for investigative work, and robust fact-checking mechanisms, we can reverse the tide.

As we strive toward making Bharat Vishwaguru, it is our responsibility to ensure that the media remains free, independent, and accountable. The solutions proposed here, though challenging, are essential steps toward restoring public confidence in the media. By empowering both the press and the people, we create a healthier, more transparent democracy—one that is truly worthy of global leadership.

Together, we can build a media landscape that upholds truth and serves the greater good of the nation. This, in turn, will help us solidify our place as a global thought leader—Vishwaguru—and protect the core democratic values that have defined India for centuries.

CHAPTER THIRTY-FIVE

GROWING INFLUENCE OF FAKE NEWS

As I reflect on the challenges confronting our great nation, one issue stands out with alarming prominence: the growing influence of fake news. In our digital age, misinformation spreads faster than ever, often with devastating consequences. This chapter delves into how fake news has emerged as a potent tool for spreading misinformation, leading to communal violence, political instability, and a profound distrust of credible media sources. Addressing this issue is not just a matter of correcting falsehoods but is crucial for safeguarding the integrity of our society and fostering the environment needed to achieve our vision of India as Vishwaguru—a global leader. The urgency of combating fake news aligns directly with our aspiration to build a nation where truth prevails and progress thrives.

Problem:

The proliferation of fake news has become a significant threat to the social fabric of India. In recent years, we've witnessed how fabricated stories can incite communal violence, disrupt social harmony, and undermine democratic processes. A stark example of this was the 2018 Assam riots, where fake news about child abductions circulated through social media, resulting in several deaths and widespread panic. According to a report by the Internet and Mobile Association of India (IAMAI), over 65% of Indians have encountered fake news on social media, reflecting a severe problem of misinformation that is affecting millions.

Another example is the 2020 Delhi riots, which were exacerbated by provocative and misleading information shared on various platforms. A study by the Data and Society Research Institute found that misinformation played a crucial role in escalating tensions and violence during these events. Fake news not only distorts public perception but also undermines trust in legitimate news sources, creating a cycle of skepticism and confusion.

The historical context of fake news is not new; however, the digital age has amplified its reach and impact. The 2002 Gujarat riots, for instance, saw the use of biased and sensationalist media to inflame tensions. This pattern of misinformation has evolved, with social media now acting as a catalyst for rapid dissemination, making it even harder to control and correct false narratives.

Solutions according to Varad Tikam

Legislative Measures:

A robust legal framework is essential for combating fake news. We should introduce a comprehensive law that addresses the creation, dissemination, and impact of false information. This law should include stringent penalties for those found guilty of deliberately spreading fake news, with clear definitions and guidelines to prevent misuse. A draft proposal might look like this:

"An Act to Prevent the Dissemination of Misinformation: This Act aims to establish a legal framework to deter the creation and spread of false

information. Any individual or entity found to be deliberately spreading misinformation shall be subject to penalties, including fines and imprisonment. The Act shall also empower regulatory bodies to monitor and address instances of fake news."

Challenges to this approach include ensuring that the law is not used to stifle free speech. To address this, the legislation should include safeguards to protect legitimate dissent and criticism.

Technological Solutions:

Leveraging technology to detect and flag fake news is another critical solution. Collaborating with tech companies to develop advanced algorithms that can identify and counteract misinformation in real-time can be effective. Platforms like Facebook and Twitter already use such technology to some extent, but more rigorous measures are needed. For example, incorporating AI-powered systems that analyze the credibility of sources and the content of news can help filter out false information.

Public Awareness and Education:

Educating the public about media literacy is crucial. Initiatives should focus on teaching people how to critically assess information and recognize fake news. Schools and universities should incorporate media literacy into their curricula, and public awareness campaigns should be launched to inform citizens about the dangers of misinformation.

Strengthening Journalistic Standards:

Reinforcing the standards of journalism and supporting investigative reporting can also play a significant role. Encouraging media outlets to adhere to ethical practices and verifying the credibility of their sources will help restore trust in traditional news sources.

International Collaboration:

Fake news is a global issue and requires international cooperation. Sharing best practices and collaborating on cross-border efforts to address misinformation can enhance the effectiveness of national measures

Conclusion

As I conclude this chapter, I reflect on the immense responsibility we bear in tackling the issue of fake news. The solutions presented are not merely theoretical but practical steps that, if implemented effectively, can lead to a more informed and cohesive society. By enacting legislative reforms, embracing technological advancements, promoting media literacy, and reinforcing journalistic standards, we can combat misinformation and build a more trustworthy media environment.

Our commitment to addressing fake news is integral to our broader vision of making India Vishwaguru. It is a testament to our dedication to truth, progress, and global leadership. As we move forward, let us embrace these challenges with determination and resolve, ensuring that our nation's future is grounded in integrity and shared values.

CHAPTER THIRTY-SIX

THE SILENT CRISIS MENTAL HEALTH

As I write this chapter, I cannot help but ponder the growing urgency around mental health in India. Our nation is often focused on physical ailments, while mental health remains a silent crisis. In our pursuit of becoming Vishwaguru, a global leader, it is critical to address not just the physical, but the mental well-being of our people. Mental health impacts everything—from productivity to social harmony to the very quality of life we seek to improve for every Indian citizen. Ignoring this critical aspect is no longer an option if we truly want to build a prosperous, future-ready nation.

Mental health challenges are pervasive, affecting millions of Indians regardless of their socio-economic background. Yet, due to a lack of infrastructure, awareness, and trained professionals, many people suffer in silence, untreated and often misunderstood. If we are to create a better future for India, we must act now to build a robust mental health system. In this chapter, I will explore practical solutions that can address our mental health crisis and help pave the way toward a healthier and more compassionate society.

Problem: Lack of Infrastructure and Professional Support

The core issue begins with the absence of accessible mental health services in many parts of the country. Aligarh, a small town in northern India, is home to over 200,000 people, yet there is not a single mental health clinic within a 50-kilometer radius. For residents of such areas, the prospect of getting mental health care is almost non-existent. The few urban centers that offer mental health services are either too expensive or overstretched, with wait times of months to see a psychiatrist. This severe shortage has left millions of Indians without the care they need.

Solution: Expanding Mental Health Services through Telemedicine and District Clinics

To address this gap, one of the most practical solutions is establishing mental health clinics at the district level. Every district should have its dedicated clinic staffed with qualified mental health professionals such as psychiatrists, psychologists, and counselors. These centers should be integrated into the general healthcare system, ensuring that anyone who seeks medical help for physical issues can also be screened for mental health concerns.

Telemedicine offers an immediate solution to reach areas that lack mental health professionals. The government must invest in building a robust telemedicine platform that connects rural communities with psychiatrists and psychologists in urban centers. Take, for example, the success of telemedicine in Karnataka, where community health workers help rural patients consult with psychiatrists via video calls. If such a system can be implemented nationwide, people in even the most remote corners of the country will be able to access quality mental health care. By doing this, we not only bridge the gap between rural and urban health infrastructure, but we also make mental health services more affordable and accessible.

However, expanding access alone isn't enough. We must ensure that these services are affordable for the common man. Mental health care should be included in all government health schemes such as Ayushman Bharat. People should not have to choose between feeding their families and seeking treatment for mental illness.

Problem: Stigma and Lack of Awareness

Mental health is often misunderstood and stigmatized, especially in rural areas. Imagine a family in Lucknow, where a young girl named Ayesha is experiencing severe depression. Her parents think she's simply "acting out" or possessed by evil spirits. They take her to local healers, further delaying her access to proper medical care. This story is not unique; in countless towns and villages across India, families remain unaware of mental health issues and often resort to unscientific, harmful methods to "cure" their loved ones.

Solution: Awareness Campaigns and Mental Health Education in Schools

Education is the cornerstone of erasing stigma. We need a national-level awareness campaign akin to Swachh Bharat to change how people view mental health. In this campaign, celebrities, sports figures, and influencers from all walks of life should come forward to talk about mental health struggles openly. Imagine a campaign led by well-known cricketers or Bollywood stars explaining that seeking help for mental illness is as important as getting treated for a physical disease.

This awareness must also extend into our educational system. Mental health education should be incorporated into school curriculums, starting as early as middle school. Teachers and school counselors must be trained to identify early signs of mental health issues in students and take the necessary steps to offer help. Workshops on stress management, emotional well-being, and dealing with anxiety should become a standard part of every child's education.

Additionally, peer-to-peer support programs can be initiated, where students are trained in basic mental health first aid to help their classmates cope with stress, anxiety, or any signs of emotional distress. This would encourage students to talk about their feelings without fear of being judged or ostracized.

Problem: Shortage of Trained Mental Health Professionals

One of the most critical barriers to improving mental health infrastructure in India is the severe shortage of trained professionals. Currently, India has fewer than 9,000 psychiatrists for a population of over 1.4 billion people, far below the World Health Organization's recommended ratio of 1 psychiatrist per 100,000 individuals. In small towns like Varanasi, there are often no mental health professionals available for miles. This shortage is crippling our ability to address mental health challenges effectively.

Solution: Boosting the Training of Mental Health Professionals

To overcome this shortage, we must dramatically increase the number of mental health professionals in the country. The government should offer incentives, including scholarships and loan forgiveness programs, to encourage students to pursue careers in psychiatry, psychology, and social work. The inclusion of mental health training as a mandatory part of medical education is essential. General practitioners must receive basic training in mental health so that they can diagnose and treat common disorders like anxiety and depression at the primary care level.

We can also train and mobilize a new generation of community health workers, focusing on mental health care. These workers can be given basic training to identify symptoms of mental health issues and provide preliminary care, referring serious cases to specialists. Imagine an army of mental health workers reaching every village and town, offering early intervention and guidance. This grassroots-level intervention will ensure that mental health services are available even in remote areas.

Solution: Leveraging Technology for Early Detection and Support

In today's world, technology can be a game-changer for mental health support. We must invest in mobile apps and AI-driven platforms that can offer counseling services, mental health screenings, and immediate support to those in need. Take the example of Priya, a 21-year-old college student who begins experiencing anxiety attacks but is too ashamed to seek help. Through a government-approved mobile app, she could access immediate counseling and schedule virtual appointments with professionals.

Such platforms can also send reminders and nudges to users, offering them mindfulness exercises, breathing techniques, and other self-help tools. They can play a significant role in offering continuous support, especially for individuals who are hesitant to visit a clinic or hospital in person. With India's expanding smartphone user base, such technological interventions could reach millions who are otherwise disconnected from formal mental health services.

Legislative Support

A reform of this magnitude cannot be accomplished without legislative backing. The existing Mental Health Care Act (2017) needs to be expanded and made more actionable. For instance, the act currently emphasizes patient rights and decriminalizes suicide but lacks provisions to tackle the infrastructural gaps. I propose a revised version of the Mental Health Care Act that mandates district-level mental health facilities and telemedicine infrastructure.

The government must also set aside a significant portion of the national health budget specifically for mental health care. Every public and private institution with more than 500 employees should be required by law to employ a full-time mental health professional, ensuring that workplace stress and anxiety are addressed as part of employee welfare programs.

Mental health screening should be made a mandatory part of all government health schemes, ensuring that mental health care becomes as accessible as physical health services. Regular mental health check-ups could be included in routine medical care, ensuring early detection of potential issues.

Conclusion

India's mental health crisis is a complex challenge, but it is not insurmountable. If we are to become the Vishwaguru, a beacon of knowledge and wisdom for the world, we must first take care of the minds and hearts of our own people. The solutions I have proposed—from building mental health infrastructure at the district level to leveraging telemedicine, raising awareness, and training more professionals—are within our reach.

The time to act is now. By taking bold steps today, we can ensure that every Indian, whether in a remote village or a bustling city, has access to quality mental health care. Let us not wait for another generation to suffer in silence. Let us build a nation where mental health is treated with the same seriousness as physical health, where every individual has the opportunity to live a life of dignity, well-being, and fulfillment.

India's future as a global leader depends on the mental well-being of its people. Together, we can build a stronger, more compassionate nation.

CHAPTER THIRTY-SEVEN

MISMANAGEMENT OF THE HEALTH SECTOR IN INDIA

As I reflect on the current state of our nation, one issue that stands out for its urgency and direct impact on our vision of making India a global leader is the alarming mismanagement of our healthcare system. Today, millions of our fellow citizens suffer not just from illnesses, but from the system itself — a system that is underfunded, overstretched, and lacks both efficiency and empathy. I believe that addressing this issue is not only essential for the well-being of our people but also critical for positioning India as *Vishwaguru* — a leader in knowledge, compassion, and innovation. We cannot aspire to lead the world if we cannot adequately care for our own.

India's healthcare sector holds immense potential, yet it is burdened by a myriad of challenges. The current framework is one that denies access to quality healthcare for millions, particularly in rural areas. The country's inadequate investment in public health and the poor management of government hospitals have led to overcrowding, mismanagement, and, in many cases, disastrous outcomes for those who depend on it. If we are to ensure a future where India truly shines on the world stage, we must begin with reforms in how we treat the health of our citizens. Our people are the backbone of our nation; their health must be our priority.

The Problem: A Failing Healthcare System

The roots of India's healthcare crisis lie in its persistent underfunding. India spends just about 1.28% of its GDP on healthcare, which is far below the global average of 6% . This chronic underfunding has resulted in dilapidated public hospitals, with insufficient staff, outdated equipment, and inadequate facilities. Government-run hospitals, often the only option for the vast majority of Indians, are overwhelmed with patients. One heartbreaking example of this is the Gorakhpur tragedy in 2017, where over 60 children died in a government hospital due to a lack of oxygen supplies . This incident exposes the grim reality of mismanagement, where even life-saving resources were mishandled, resulting in preventable deaths.

Further compounding the problem is the unregulated growth of private healthcare in India. While private hospitals offer world-class treatment, they are financially out of reach for a majority of the population. According to the National Sample Survey (NSS), nearly 80% of healthcare costs in India are borne out-of-pocket by patients and their families . This leads to many families being pushed below the poverty line due to medical expenses. Moreover, there is a significant gap between urban and rural healthcare infrastructure, leaving rural populations vulnerable and underserved.

Real-life stories of individuals who suffer under this system are countless. Take the case a 32-year-old mother from Bihar, who died from complications during childbirth in a government hospital due to a lack of basic medical attention and infrastructure. Her case is not an anomaly but a representation of the healthcare crisis that is gripping the entire nation. Such tragedies highlight how our healthcare system is not just under strain but is failing.

Solutions according to Varad Tikam

Increased Public Health Investment

We need a significant and sustained increase in public health funding. The government must raise its healthcare expenditure from the current 1.28% of GDP to at least 5% within the next five years. This funding will go towards upgrading public hospitals, recruiting more medical professionals, and ensuring that rural areas have access to healthcare services. Countries like Thailand, which achieved universal health coverage by focusing on public sector healthcare reforms, offer a model that India can follow . Increased investment will help tackle overcrowding in hospitals and ensure that every citizen receives basic care without having to bankrupt themselves.

Regulating Private Healthcare

Private hospitals should not be profit-driven entities at the expense of patients' health. It is essential to establish a robust regulatory framework that limits the exorbitant pricing practices currently seen in the private sector. There should be a cap on how much hospitals can charge for treatments, and the government must enforce transparency in healthcare costs. In addition, we should introduce mandatory price controls on essential treatments and procedures, ensuring that lifesaving healthcare remains affordable to all. This will require collaboration between the government, healthcare professionals, and industry leaders to find a balanced approach that benefits both patients and hospitals.

Universal Health Coverage (UHC)

We must prioritize the implementation of universal health coverage in India. This will ensure that every citizen, regardless of income level, has access to affordable healthcare. The government's flagship Ayushman Bharat program has been a step in the right direction, but it must be expanded to cover more people and provide more comprehensive services. Under UHC, preventive care should be made a cornerstone, with a focus on early diagnosis and treatment to reduce the burden of diseases. If the UHC system is well implemented, it could save millions from poverty due to medical expenses.

Rural Healthcare Infrastructure

One of the most critical areas for reform is the healthcare infrastructure in rural areas. The government must ensure that primary healthcare centers (PHCs) in rural areas are well-equipped and staffed with qualified doctors and nurses. Telemedicine can play a significant role in bridging the healthcare gap in these areas. By leveraging technology, rural populations can access specialist consultations without having to travel to urban centers. In addition, mobile healthcare units can be introduced to reach remote and underserved populations, ensuring that no citizen is left behind.

Medical Education Reform

The shortage of doctors, particularly in rural areas, is a critical issue. To address this, we need to reform medical education in India. Medical colleges should focus on producing more general practitioners and rural health specialists who are incentivized to work in underserved areas. Furthermore, the government should introduce scholarships and loan forgiveness programs for students who commit to serving in rural and underprivileged communities for a certain period after their graduation. This will help bridge the gap between the number of healthcare providers and the demand for healthcare services.

Digitizing Healthcare Records

One significant reform would be to introduce a national digital health record system. By digitizing patient records, we can ensure that healthcare providers have access to accurate patient histories, reducing medical errors and improving patient care. A centralized digital system would also allow the government to track disease outbreaks more efficiently, enabling better management of public health crises

Conclusion

India's healthcare crisis is one of the most significant challenges facing our nation today. However, I am confident that with bold reforms and unwavering commitment, we can turn this crisis into an opportunity to build a healthcare system that not only serves our people but also stands as a model for the world. As we strive to make India *Vishwaguru*, it is vital that we recognize that the health of our people forms the foundation of our national strength. A healthy population is the backbone of a prosperous, innovative, and thriving nation. The time for change is now, and with the proposed solutions, I believe we can lead India into a future where healthcare is a right, not a privilege.

India's rise as a global leader must begin with its people — and their well-being. Together, we can create a nation that cares for its citizens, providing them with the healthcare they deserve.

"Let this be our first step toward the India of tomorrow — an India that is not just a leader in words, but in action."

CHAPTER THIRTY-EIGHT

STRATEGIC BLUEPRINT FOR RAW

Strategic Blueprint for India's Research and Analysis Wing (RAW)

In a world defined by shifting power dynamics, emerging technologies, and unpredictable threats, the role of intelligence agencies has never been more critical. As India stands on the cusp of becoming a global power, the responsibility of safeguarding our nation's interests, both within and beyond our borders, falls heavily on the Research and Analysis Wing (RAW). This chapter delves into the strategic imperatives that guide RAW's operations, offering a comprehensive plan to ensure that India not only navigates but also thrives in this complex international landscape.

From the crowded streets of South Asia to the resource-rich terrains of Africa, India's influence must be carefully cultivated and protected. We are surrounded by challenges—rising regional powers, enduring conflicts, and the constant specter of terrorism. In response, RAW's mission must be both expansive and precise, aiming to neutralize threats before they reach our doorstep while simultaneously advancing India's strategic goals on the global stage.

This chapter is not merely a theoretical exploration; it is a call to action. The strategies outlined herein are designed to fortify India's position in an increasingly competitive world, ensuring that our nation is not just a participant in global affairs, but a leader. Through meticulous planning, intelligence gathering, and covert operations, RAW can and must be the sentinel that guards India's future, shaping the destiny of a nation poised for greatness.

As we explore the specifics of this strategic plan, it is essential to recognize that these are not just policies—they are the pillars upon which India's security and sovereignty rest. This introduction sets the stage for a detailed examination of the actions required to secure our nation's place in the world, and the profound importance of each decision that RAW makes in the service of India.

1. Identifying Strategic Regions and Countries

1. South Asia: The Immediate Periphery

In South Asia, India's immediate periphery comprises a diverse and complex set of relationships with neighboring countries. Addressing these relationships requires a nuanced approach blending intelligence operations, diplomatic maneuvering, and cultural engagement.

Pakistan: The enduring challenge posed by Pakistan necessitates a multifaceted strategy. The primary focus would be on intelligence penetration. By deploying deep-cover agents within Pakistan's political, military, and terrorist networks, India can gather actionable intelligence. This intelligence will be instrumental in anticipating and neutralizing hostile actions before they materialize. Concurrently, influence operations will play a critical role in destabilizing Pakistan's internal dynamics. Disinformation campaigns aimed at creating political and social divisions within Pakistan can weaken its government's capacity to support anti-India activities. On the ground, cross-border surveillance using advanced technologies like drones and satellites will be crucial in monitoring border areas, particularly in Kashmir, to detect and prevent terrorist infiltration or military mobilization.

Bangladesh: In Bangladesh, the approach involves counter-radicalization efforts. Collaboration with Bangladeshi intelligence agencies will focus on monitoring and disrupting radicalization networks. Joint operations can target extremist groups and their funding sources. Economically, leveraging India's substantial trade ties with Bangladesh can help influence key infrastructure projects to align with Indian strategic interests, while simultaneously countering Chinese investments that could shift regional power balances.

Nepal: For Nepal, political engagement and cultural diplomacy will be the cornerstones of India's strategy. Building relationships with influential political figures across party lines, including providing covert financial support to pro-India factions, will ensure favorable policies. Cultural diplomacy will involve promoting Indian culture and values through educational exchanges and cultural programs to foster a positive sentiment toward India.

Sri Lanka and Bhutan: In Sri Lanka, maritime surveillance initiatives will be crucial. By establishing joint surveillance operations, India and Sri Lanka can monitor Chinese naval activities in the Indian Ocean, ensuring maritime security. For Bhutan, supporting infrastructure development that enhances connectivity with India will counterbalance Chinese-funded projects and solidify India's strategic foothold in the region.

2. Southeast Asia: Counterbalancing China

Myanmar: India's strategy in Myanmar will focus on counterinsurgency collaboration. Providing training and intelligence support to the Myanmar military can help address insurgent threats along the India-Myanmar border. Diplomatic efforts will aim to ensure Myanmar's neutrality or support in dealings with China, potentially through economic incentives or security assurances.

Vietnam and Indonesia: Strengthening defense cooperation with Vietnam and Indonesia will be crucial in countering Chinese influence in the South China Sea. This includes joint military exercises and intelligence sharing on Chinese activities. Maritime security initiatives will involve establishing monitoring stations to track Chinese naval movements and protect crucial sea lanes.

3. The Middle East: Securing Energy and Countering Extremism

Iran, Saudi Arabia, and UAE: India's approach in the Middle East will revolve around energy diplomacy and counterterrorism partnerships. By anticipating shifts in global energy markets and negotiating long-term contracts, India can secure stable energy supplies. Concurrently, intelligence-sharing agreements with these countries will facilitate monitoring and disrupting terrorist networks that pose a threat to Indian interests.

Monitoring Extremism: Surveillance of extremist movements within these countries will be essential. Deploying human intelligence (HUMINT) assets to infiltrate communities and organizations suspected of harboring extremist sympathies will enable preemptive disruption of plots against India.

4. Africa: The Next Frontier

Nigeria, South Africa, and Kenya: In Africa, establishing intelligence outposts to monitor and secure access to critical resources will be vital. Engaging in covert diplomacy to counteract Chinese influence and building relationships with key political and military leaders will help secure pro-India policies and investment opportunities.

5. Counterterrorism Operations

Pakistan: Counter-insurgency operations within Pakistan will involve infiltrating militant groups and utilizing gathered intelligence to launch targeted strikes. Information warfare strategies will include disinformation campaigns to discredit terrorist organizations both domestically and internationally.

Afghanistan: To prevent extremist resurgence in Afghanistan, India will focus on building alliances with local leaders and tribal chiefs opposed to extremism. Covert intelligence operations will monitor extremist movements and track financial transactions to identify safe-havens.

Middle East & North Africa: Disrupting terrorist networks in the Middle East and North Africa involves tracing and disrupting the flow of funds to terrorist organizations through financial intelligence (FININT) operations. Covert operations to sabotage arms shipments will prevent these groups from acquiring necessary resources.

6. Cyber Operations

China and Pakistan: In the cyber domain, India will develop advanced malware and espionage tools to penetrate Chinese and Pakistani critical infrastructures, gathering intelligence on military, economic, and security operations. Strengthening India's cyber defense through AI and machine learning technologies will enhance the capability to detect and neutralize cyber threats in real-time.

Global Reach: Establishing a global cyber intelligence network with centers in key regions will enable comprehensive monitoring of global cyber threats. Offensive cyber capabilities will be developed to launch retaliatory attacks against adversaries, potentially targeting critical infrastructure and communication networks.

7. Political Influence and Diplomacy

South Asia: To shape political outcomes, India will covertly fund political parties and candidates aligned with its interests. Media manipulation strategies will use state and private media to promote narratives favorable to India and discredit opposition.

Global South: Enhancing India's soft power through cultural diplomacy initiatives and strategic partnerships with key countries in Africa, Latin America, and Asia will position India as a leader in the Global South. This includes promoting Indian culture, education, and technology and focusing on shared goals like economic development and counterterrorism.

Countering Hostile Nations: Diplomatic campaigns will highlight Pakistan's links to global terrorism, presenting evidence at international forums and lobbying for diplomatic isolation. Sanction advocacy will target the financial systems and military capabilities of nations supporting terrorism.

8. Economic Intelligence and Operations

China: Countering the Belt and Road Initiative (BRI) involves gathering intelligence on BRI projects and proposing alternative projects to counter Chinese influence. Economic sabotage may be employed where feasible to disrupt or delay BRI initiatives.

Energy Security: Establishing a unit within RAW to monitor global energy markets will provide real-time intelligence on supply disruptions and price fluctuations. Securing long-term energy contracts and negotiating deals with emerging energy producers will ensure stable energy supplies.

Technology Acquisition: Covert operations to acquire advanced technologies from global innovators will enhance India's strategic capabilities. Counter-espionage measures will protect India's technological innovations from foreign intelligence threats.

9. Human Intelligence (HUMINT) Networks

Diaspora: Leveraging global Indian communities will involve establishing intelligence networks within the diaspora to gather information on local developments affecting India. Using the diaspora for soft power will promote Indian culture and counter anti-India narratives.

Recruitment: Targeted recruitment programs will infiltrate hostile entities by identifying potential recruits through social networks, financial incentives, or ideological alignment. Extensive training and incentives will be provided to ensure the effectiveness of recruited assets.

This strategic framework outlines a comprehensive approach to addressing India's national security concerns, balancing immediate and long-term objectives across diverse regions and domains.

Conclusion

As I draw this chapter to a close, I am reminded of the immense responsibility that rests on the shoulders of India's intelligence community, particularly the Research and Analysis Wing (RAW). The strategic plan outlined here is not merely a blueprint for foreign engagement; it is a roadmap for securing India's future in an increasingly volatile and competitive global landscape.

From the intricate web of alliances and rivalries in South Asia to the strategic balancing act required in Southeast Asia and the Middle East, each component of this plan is crucial for safeguarding our national interests. The world is evolving rapidly, and so are the threats that challenge our security and prosperity. Terrorism, cyber warfare, economic espionage, and geopolitical power plays are no longer isolated events—they are interconnected forces that can have far-reaching consequences for our nation.

The importance of this plan cannot be overstated. It is not just about responding to immediate threats; it is about building a resilient and proactive intelligence apparatus that can anticipate and mitigate dangers before they materialize. It is about securing our borders, influencing global outcomes in our favor, and ensuring that India remains a dominant force on the world stage.

As an author, I understand that this plan is ambitious, but ambition is the bedrock of progress. By implementing these strategies, RAW can effectively counter adversaries, protect our people, and promote India's vision of a peaceful and prosperous world. The stakes are high, and the path ahead is fraught with challenges, but with a plan like this, we can ensure that India not only survives but thrives in the face of global uncertainties. This is not just a plan for RAW; it is a plan for India's future, and its success is vital for the nation's security, sovereignty, and standing in the world.

Conclusion

As we conclude BluePrint to Make Bharat Vishwaguru, it's clear that this vision is a call to action for our nation's future. This book has explored key challenges and proposed solutions to elevate Bharat to global prominence. From education reform to national security, each proposal aims to strengthen our nation and align with our core values.

I extend my heartfelt thanks to *Shakti (universe)* for the guidance and inspiration that made this book possible and for helping me develop these solutions at such a young age. If any errors or statements have caused unintended offense, I offer my sincere apologies. My goal is always to foster constructive dialogue and progress.

Achieving this vision requires collective effort and dedication. By embracing these ideas, we can work towards making Bharat a beacon of innovation and leadership on the world stage.

Thank you for joining me on this journey. Together, let's turn this vision into reality and make Bharat a global leader.

"Success is not the destination but the journey of transforming challenges into opportunities and dreams into reality. Keep moving forward, for each step brings us closer to greatness"